PRINCELY RAJASTHAN

RAJPUT PALACES AND MANSIONS

PRINCELY RAJASTHAN

RAJPUT PALACES AND MANSIONS

Antonio Martinelli & George Michell

PRINCELY RAJASTHAN

RAJPUT PALACES AND MANSIONS

WITH Aman Nath

THE VENDOME PRESS

CONTENTS

MAHARAJA TAKHT SINGH, 1843.

MAHARAJA JASWANT SINGH II., G.C.S.I. 1873.

MAHARAJA SARDAR SINGH, SUCCEEDED IN 1895.

1211
12   „ RIR MAL, 1417.
13   „ JODHAJI, 1453.
14   „ SUJA, 1491.
15   „ UDAI SINGH.
        (DID NOT REIGN).
16   „ GANGA, 1515.
17   „ MALDEO, 1531.
18   „ UDAI SINGH
        (THE MOTA RAJA), 1583.
19   RAJA SUR SINGH, 1594.
20   „ SAJ SINGH, 101.
21   ARAJA JASWANT
        SINGH I., 1635.
22   „ AJIT SINGH, 1678.
23   „ ABHI SINGH, 1725.
24   „ RAM SINGH, 1750.
25   „ BAKHT SINGH, 1751.
26   „ BIJAI SINGH, 1753.
27   „ BHEEM SINGH, 1794.
28   „ MAN SINGH, 1804.

१ राव सियाजी. संन. १२११.
२. „ रिमल, „ १२९९.
१३ „ जोधाजी, „ १४५३.
१४ „ सूजा, „ १४९१.
१५ „ उदेसिंघ.
      (राज न्हांकीया).
१६ „ राजा, „ १५१५.
१७ „ माःदेव, „ १५३१.
१८ „ रःदासंघ.
      (मोटा राजा), १५८३.
१९ राजा सुरसिंघ, „ १५९४.
२० „ साजसिंघ, „ १६१४.
२१ म्हाराजा जसवंतसिंघ
      १. सन् १६३५.
२२ „ अजीतसिंघ, १६७८.
२३ „ अभैसिंघ, १७२५.
२४ „ रामसिंघ, १७५०.
२५ „ वषतसिंघ, „ १७५१.
२६ „ विजैसिंघ, „ १७५३.
२७ „ भीमसिंघ, १७९४.
२८ „ मानसिंघ, १८०४.
२९ „ तषतसिंघ, १८४३.
३० जसवंतसिंघ २.,
      जी.सी.एस.आई.सन् १८७३.
३१.   सरदारसिंघ,
      काभराबहुये. सन् १८९५.

INTRODUCTION

HISTORICAL BACKGROUND

Traditionally known as Rajputana, Land of the Rajputs, the arid desert state of Rajasthan in north-western India is home to noble warrior families of the Hindu Kshatriya caste such as the Sisodias of Chittaurgarh (Chittor) and Udaipur, the Rathors of Jodhpur, and the Kachhawahas of Amber and Jaipur. Though these and other Rajput dynasties wielded considerable influence over the last five hundred years or so, no single line ever came to dominate the entire region during this period. Thus, the history of Rajasthan is that of different kingdoms coexisting uneasily, competing for territories and resources, and sometimes fragmenting into smaller, but equally quarrelsome states. At the height of the Mughal rule in the 17th century, this inter-Rajput rivalry abated, but it was only with the British conquest of north India in the early 19th century that it finally came to an end, and a period of peace descended over this strife-torn region.

Many Rajput dynasties trace their lineage back one thousand years and more, if not beyond into the realm of myth. Even so, most of the ruling families that survive into the modern era do not enter history until the 15th century, a time when much of Rajasthan was under the control of the Delhi sultans and their contemporaries in Gujarat, immediately south of Rajasthan, and Malwa, to the south-east. Yet, several Rajput warriors managed to defy sultanate supremacy. Rana Kumbha of the illustrious Sisodia family built up the fortresses at Chittaurgarh and Kumbhalgarh into prominent bastions of Rajput strength, while Rao Jodha, founder of the Jodhpur kingdom, set himself up as an independent ruler. Such efforts to affirm Rajput autonomy, however, met with stiff resistance from the sultans.

In the second half of the 16th century, the invading Mughals rapidly established themselves as the supreme power in north India. Under the leadership of the young but capable Akbar (1556-1605), the Mughal army conquered the kingdoms of the Delhi, Gujarat and Malwa sultans. Buoyed by these victories, Akbar then turned to Rajasthan, overwhelming the Rajputs by sheer military force. His successful siege and capture in 1568 of Chittaurgarh, the greatest fortress of Rajasthan, marked a turning point in the region's history; after this victory, gaining control over the remaining Rajput kingdoms was relatively easy, and the Rajputs were forcibly persuaded to acknowledge Mughal hegemony. A notable exception was Mewar, home of the Sisodias, who by this time had abandoned Chittaurgarh for their new capital at Udaipur, and still maintained some measure of independence. It was not until 1614, during the reign of the next Mughal emperor, Jahangir (1605-27), that Rana Amar Singh I of Mewar formally submitted. After securing his victories in Rajasthan, Akbar went on to pursue a policy of conciliation by employing Rajput rulers as commanders and governors in his rapidly expanding empire, and taking Rajput princesses as wives. From the Rajput point of view, an alliance with the Mughals was advantageous: it removed the distractions and expenses of internecine warfare, and at the same time offered opportunities for reward and advancement at the Mughal court. Among the first maharajas to attain high positions under Akbar and Jahangir were Man Singh of Amber, Rattan Singh of Bundi, Gaj Singh of Jodhpur, and Rai Singh of Bikaner. These rulers spent the greater part of their careers consolidating the Mughal hold on eastern India and the Deccan in peninsular India. As the 17th century progressed, and the Mughal empire reached the zenith of its extent and authority, the Rajput kingdoms benefited from an unprecedented period of peace and prosperity under rulers such as Mirza Jai Singh of Amber, Jagat Singh of Udaipur, Jaswant Singh of Jodhpur, and Anup Singh of Bikaner.

At the turn of the 18th century, the most powerful Rajput ruler in the service of the Mughals was Maharaja Sawai Jai Singh II of Jaipur. His move in 1727 from fortified Amber in the Aravalli Hills to the newly laid out city of Jaipur in the nearby plains may be interpreted as a gesture of defiance in the face of waning Mughal power. In the years that followed, inter-Rajput rivalry broke out once again as the Mughal empire began to crumble under a series of weak emperors. Crippled by battles, Rajasthan offered little resistance to the Maratha armies from Maharashtra and the local Jats who plundered the Rajput domains repeatedly in the second half of the 18th century. (The Jats were non-Rajput warriors who by this time had established themselves as rulers in eastern Rajasthan.) This unfortunate situation was only brought under control in the early 19th century when the forces of the British East India Company, acting in their own interests, vanquished the Marathas and subdued the Jats. In 1818, the Company compelled most of the maharajas to sign treaties that guaranteed protection from outside aggression, but deprived them of military independence. Complaince was ensured by an agent of the Company, known as a Resident, who was posted at the courts of different kingdoms. Thereafter, the Rajput rulers came under the scrutiny of their British Residents, who supervised their education and encouraged them to introduce progressive reforms in order to modernize their kingdoms. The most celebrated of these Residents was Colonel James Tod, whose *Annals and Antiquities of Rajasthan* remains the classic account of Rajput history. When deemed necessary, the British did not hesitate to intervene in local affairs, sometimes forcing the resignation of certain maharajas they considered incompetent, and installing others of their own choice. Where there was no male descendant, royal families adopted infant sons of their remote relatives, but only with the approval of the ever-vigilant British.

In due course, the maharajas of Rajasthan became the greatest champions of British causes, visiting London, receiving government dignitaries, entertaining foreign guests on hunting expeditions, and contributing troops to the World Wars. Outstanding figures in this regard were Madho Singh of Jaipur, Fateh Singh of Udaipur, Pratap Singh of Jodhpur, and Ganga Singh of Bikaner. These rulers and their contemporaries were also prominent members of the Chamber of Princes, a forum convened in 1921, enabling the Rajput rulers and other royal figures to discuss matters of common concern. This largely fruitful relationship between the Rajputs and the British came to an abrupt end with India's independence in 1947. Soon after, the Rajput rulers signed the Instrument of Accession whereby their dominions ceded to the Indian Union; in 1949 the modern state of Rajasthan came into existence, with Jaipur as its capital. By the time India's prime minister, Indira Gandhi, abolished the princely privileges in 1971, most descendants of the Rajput royal families had taken up careers in business, or converted their assets into charitable trusts. In the years since, they have responded to the growth of tourism in Rajasthan by transforming their palaces into hotels. Some have also achieved prominence in local politics, thereby preserving the traditional Rajput qualities of leadership and public service.

COURTLY LIFE

Life within the palaces of Rajasthan inevitably revolved around the maharaja. He was the central figure in the court's public ceremonies, as well as the head of the army, chief progenitor of the royal line, and principal worshipper of the deity who offered divine protection to his family. Surrounded by guards, retainers, nobles, commanders and other officers, the Rajput ruler was a highly visible figure. Little wonder, then, that his palace was intended as an architectural setting that affirmed the divinely ordained supremacy of the royal person. Yet, the ritualized routines of courtly life permitted the king to participate in a more private world where he could relax in the company of his male companions, children, wives and concubines.

Most Rajput maharajas were preoccupied with internecine struggles to secure their lands and expand their dominions. The monarch had to ensure that his troops and animals were adequately equipped and trained; accordingly, a part of each day was set aside for inspection and review. These activities took place in the outermost *chowk* (courtyard) of the palace. A ceremonial gateway, often with a chamber on top for drummers and other musicians, provided entry to the *chowk*, allowing soldiers and animals to pass through. Barracks for troops as well as stables and stores were located nearby. The ruler spent a significant part of the day with his commanders and generals, many of who were leading *thakurs* (landed nobles). Such assemblies, known as darbars, took place in a reception hall or canopied area within the palace. The king also appeared in a grand darbar hall, often separate from the everyday reception hall, to celebrate significant military victories or royal birthdays. At special times, he was weighed against treasures, later distributed as charity. On these and other similarly formal occasions, the maharaja received and granted gifts, signed decrees and treaties, and met with important visitors. He was seated on a *gaddi* (cushioned throne), beneath a canopy or umbrella, both ancient symbols of sovereignty. Attendants bearing flywhisks, fans, banners and other regalia stood on either side, while weapons, standards and portraits of royal ancestors were displayed on the walls behind. In front were the courtiers, *thakurs* and commanders, generally seated in rows on the floor. From the mid-19th century onwards, a British Resident would also have been present.

An essential duty of the maharaja was to worship the Hindu goddess who protected his family. A few minutes each morning were generally set aside for the king to visit the palace shrine where priests assisted him in his devotions. The ruler was also the leading celebrant at religious holidays such as Dussehra, when arms were worshipped and goats sacrificed to the all-powerful goddess Durga. Then there was Diwali, the festival of lights, which glorified Lakshmi, the goddess of wealth; and Holi, in which the king and his courtiers delighted in spraying coloured water on each other in celebration of the spring season. Performances of music and dance represented another aspect of courtly life. Whenever time permitted, the ruler and his companions retreated to an inner court, or one of the upper terraces of the palace to attend the evening entertainments. Apartments with murals and mirror decoration, known as *rang mahals* and *shish mahals* respectively, were also popular settings for such concerts. Most palaces had a profusion of galleries, balconies, terraces and open pavilions, intended as lookout points from where the maharaja, his family members and courtiers could gaze out over the surrounding landscape. Designed to catch the breeze, these features provided much-needed relief from the scorching desert heat.

Female members and children of the ruling family, together with their retinues of mostly female servants and guards, were confined to the *zenana* portions of the palace, where they lived separately from the maharaja and his male retinue. The custom of *purdah*, observed at Rajput courts, demanded that women not show themselves unveiled. Screened galleries overlooking the courtyards and halls of the palaces allowed royal women to discreetly observe the receptions held by the maharaja. *Zenanas* were divided into apartments, so each queen could be separately accommodated. Walled gardens and rooftop terraces in these residences permitted them to move about freely in the open without being noticed. The maharaja often visited the *zenana* to dine and to be entertained by his women as they sang or danced for him alone. The king would spend a night with his chosen wife or favourite concubine, privacy being ensured by the guards who stood on duty outside. Otherwise, the ruler and other male members of the royal household slept in their own apartments in another part of the palace, generally known as the *mardana*.

Courtly life in Rajasthan extended beyond the confines of the palace itself. Accompanied by his closest companions, the maharaja made excursions to the gardens that lay on the outskirts of his capital, or to island resorts in the middle of artificial lakes where feasts and pleasurable distractions would be arranged. Hunting expeditions were also popular, and the king sometimes built lodges at the edge of the royal game sanctuaries, which he maintained within his kingdoms. At auspicious times in the religious calendar, the ruler made pilgrimages to important shrines at some distance from his capital, since these represented the terrestrial homes of his family deity.

PALACE ARCHITECTURE

Given the struggles of the early Rajput warriors to establish their independence in the face of repeated assaults and invasions, it is hardly surprising that the first palaces in Rajasthan were conceived as fortified citadels. Massive ramparts strengthened by circular bastions protect the 15th-century palaces at Chittaurgarh, one of the oldest and

greatest Rajput strongholds. Mehrangarh, founded at about the same time, presents an impregnable pile of masonry rising dramatically above the city of Jodhpur. The ramp ascending to the palace within is guarded by a sequence of imposing gateways. Junagarh in Bikaner, dating from the end of the 16th century, is equally well protected by massive battlemented walls laid out in regular formation on a flat site. The contemporary Garh Palace in Bundi was also conceived as a citadel, but with fortified residential wings that step up a precipitous hill. In these examples, as in most other royal complexes in Rajasthan, the palace was protected by massive walls topped by battlements, broken only by lofty, arched gateways that were surmounted by open domed pavilions known as *chhatris*. The same battlemented walls and gateways with *chhatris* are found in the architecture of the sultans, as may be seen in the royal complexes in Delhi and Mandu (capital of Malwa) dating back to the 14th and 15th centuries, pointing to a shared military architectural tradition that was common across much of north India. Though by the 18th century there was less demand for heavily defended palaces, royal residences continued to be concealed behind high walls with towers and ceremonial gateways, as in City Palace in Jaipur.

High walls were also required for privacy, as is apparent in Rana Kumbha's Palace at Chittaurgarh. This walled complex is entered through a gateway that gives access to a *chowk* (court) overlooked by a *sabha* (columned assembly hall). A corridor leads from this public court to a number of self-contained residential apartments, each opening onto a quadrangular *chowk*. This clear demarcation of public and private zones was to remain a constant feature of Rajput palace architecture; so too the inward-looking apartments arranged around a central walled *chowk*. For instance, in the original portions of the palace at Amber and City Palace in Udaipur, both dating from the 16th century, suites of rooms on three or four levels are symmetrically disposed around a rectangular court. Apartments at the topmost levels are roofed with domes or pointed vaults, and linked by terraces lined with *chhatris*. (One of the earliest examples of this typical palace scheme, complete with rooftop *chhatris*, is Gujari Mahal built by the Tomar Rajput ruler, Man Singh, in Gwalior in central India at the beginning of the 16th century; another is the Rajput-styled palace of Jodh Bai, within the private zone of Akbar's palace city of Fatehpur Sikri, dating from the 1570s.)

As palaces came to be expanded in the course of the 17th century, they became extensive complexes with multiple *chowks*. Interior courts were disposed in a linear arrangement, as in Mehrangarh in Jodhpur and the palace at Amber, or in ascending levels, as in Udaipur's City Palace. The sequence of *chowks* in each of these complexes defines a crucial transition from public to private zones. This transition usually begins with the ceremonial gateway leading to the outermost courtyard, where the ruler would review his troops and animals, and ends with the *zenana* in the furthermost part of the palace, usually provided with its own walled courtyard. Each *chowk* within the palace is in effect a self-contained unit with inward-looking apartments, chambers and corridors disposed on multiple levels. *Jharokas* (projecting balconies) interspersed with *jalis* (openwork screens) distinguish the topmost rooms. Together with *chhatris*, such *jharokas* and *jalis* become a ubiquitous feature of Rajput royal architecture, testifying to the importance of looking down or gazing outward, whether for security or pleasure.

No doubt, the earliest palaces in Rajasthan were lavishly decorated, but sadly almost nothing survives other than fragments of coloured tiles and traces of paintings, as in Rana Kumbha's Palace at Chittaurgarh. Palaces dating from the 17th century, however, preserve a profusion of murals, carved plaster work and coloured glass inlaid work, the most typical decorative techniques of the era. Openwork *jalis* were common, and it is here that local craftsmen concentrated much of their talents. Carved out of sandstone (in imitation of wood), such screens combined intricate geometric patterns with delicacy of texture. *Jalis* were also fashioned out of plaster to create more fluid designs incorporating parrots or peacocks. Not content with filtering natural light in this manner, craftsmen sought vivid colour effects. *Jalis* were filled with coloured glass to achieve a technicolour translucency that enhanced interior apartments. Pieces of coloured glass were also set into plaster walls to create brilliant mosaic patterns, as seen in Badi Chatur Chowk of Udaipur's City Palace.

It is, however, the murals for which the palaces in Rajasthan are best known. Most interior apartments dating from the 18th and 19th centuries are covered with painted designs, many of them foliate motifs with friezes of petals and leaves, flowers and arabesque scrollwork, all realized in vibrant colours, sometimes highlighted with gold. Figural subjects are also common, especially those drawn from Hindu mythology, testifying to the vigorous pictorial tradition in this part of India. In Chitra Shala at Bundi Garh Palace, for instance, walls and ceilings are covered with scenes depicting the exploits of Krishna, including his dalliances with the *gopis* (herdswomen) particularly Radha, his favourite. Popular shrines in Rajasthan, such as the Krishna temple in the small village at Nathdwara, are also portrayed in the murals.

MUGHAL INFLUENCE

Courtly life in Rajasthan came to be profoundly influenced by Mughal ceremonial routine, dress and language, as many of Rajasthan's maharajas spent a major part of their careers in the imperial service of the Mughals. Under their influence, the maharajas developed a taste for darbars (formal receptions) in the grand Mughal style. Accordingly, 17th-century palaces in Rajasthan are often provided with columned audience halls that imitate the Diwan-i Ams in the Red Forts of Agra and Delhi, one of the most celebrated examples being that in Amber Palace. (Since such halls correspond closely to the *sabhas* found in the earliest Rajput palaces, as at Chittaurgarh, it may be argued that their appearance in Mughal architecture is an instance of Rajput influence.) The more evolved Mughal type darbar hall in 17th-century Rajput palaces comprises a double-height space lined with arcades, with a throne at one end on a slightly raised platform, and side balconies at the upper level for courtly women to witness the proceedings. Such halls were conceived as monumental settings for the display of dynastic regalia and sumptuous ornamentation. They opened onto spacious *chowks* with apartments disposed on three sides. An essential element of such halls and their adjacent courts was the Mughal-styled arch with multiple lobes, carried on columns with leafy bases and capitals.

Other Mughal elements found in 17th-century Rajput palaces are domes and vaults with ornamental ribs and facets. A novel feature is the *bangla* vault with its curved ridge and cornice, a motif that originally derived from Bengal in eastern India (hence its name), but entered the vocabulary of Mughal architecture, from where it was borrowed by the Rajputs. The *bangla* was to prove extremely popular in Rajasthan, both as a roof to crown pavilions, balconies and *chhatris*, and also as a decorative motif in shallow relief crowning a wall niche or seating alcove. Other architectural forms that were shared with the Mughals include the *hathi pol*, or ceremonial gateway with elephant brackets sculpted in three dimensions, as in the entrance to Bundi Garh Palace, and the triple-arched ceremonial gateway known as *tripolia*, seen in the outermost *chowk* of Udaipur's City Palace. Formal Persian-styled gardens were another Mughal contribution to Rajasthan's royal architecture. Interior *chowks* were transformed into walled gardens with water channels, fountains and flower-beds laid out in symmetrical geometric patterns, such as that in front of Sukh Mandir in Amber Palace. Mughal-inspired gardens also appeared in 18th-century complexes. Chandra Mahal at City Palace in Jaipur faces a grandly scaled garden, divided into squares by axial water channels with fountains. But instead of the usual pleasure pavilion or royal tomb in the middle of the garden, there is a shrine consecrated to Govindadevji, the dynastic god of the Kachhawaha maharajas. Another example of this period is the garden palace at Dig, built by the Jat rulers of Bharatpur. Here, Mughal-styled pavilions crowned with *bangla* vaults are reflected in the waters of a pair of artificial lakes that are linked by a formal garden.

The impact of Mughal architecture also extends to the interior decoration of 18th-century Rajasthan palaces. Shallow wall niches with lobed arches, used as recesses for lamps, as in Jai Mandir at Amber Palace, are obvious borrowings from Mughal practice. So too are the stylized arabesque patterns and other motifs such as flowering bushes, or vases with flowers, cut in plaster or painted in glowing colours. These designs fill wall panels and niches, and frequently the spandrels above the arches on doorways. In the hands of Rajasthani craftsmen, they become more deeply modelled and heavier in effect, though they never lose their recognizably Mughal character. Such designs are often gilded to achieve more opulent effects, as in Anup Mahal at Junagarh, Bikaner. This preference for richly coloured and shining surfaces also extends to the related technique of setting mirror into plaster walls and ceilings. The *shish mahal* of Jai Mandir in Amber Palace, with its thousands of tiny mirrored pieces set into angled facets of the vaulted ceiling, rivals and even surpasses Mughal prototypes found in the Red Forts of Agra and Lahore. That this love for reflecting surfaces became widespread in Rajasthan is demonstrated in countless mirrored interiors. Dilkhush Mahal in Udaipur's City Palace and the private apartments in Samode Palace, for example, are enhanced by cool gleaming surfaces.

Pictorial art in Rajasthan was also much influenced by Mughal traditions, as is evident from the rise of individual schools of painting at different Rajput courts during the 17th and 18th centuries. Inspired by the miniatures produced at Mughal ateliers (examples of which presumably reached the Rajput courts), artists in Rajasthan adorned the palace interiors with scenes of courtly life. Chitra Shala and

Badal Mahal in Bundi Garh Palace, and the darbar hall known as Raj Mahal in Kota Fort Palace, are enhanced with murals that portray the maharaja in his public and ceremonial roles: receiving guests in state receptions, reviewing troops, embarking on military campaigns accompanied by soldiers and animals, hunting with companions in the wooded hills beyond the city, setting out on a pilgrimage to the shrine of the family deity. More intimate scenes depict the maharaja together with his courtiers, enjoying performances of music and dance, or making love with his favourite wife or concubine. The same subjects are to be found in many other palaces in Rajasthan, notably Juna Mahal in Dungarpur.

EUROPEAN PERIOD

With the growing British influence at the Rajput courts from the mid-19th century onwards, the maharajas developed a fondness for European comforts, finding their inherited properties increasingly inconvenient. As a result, they commissioned new palaces equipped with modern amenities, but laid out in a traditional manner with clearly demarcated public and private wings, ensuring that courtly women remained confined to the *zenana*. Separate quarters were even provided for European visitors who frequented the Rajput courts. Since the new palaces were generally built on the city outskirts, they could be set in spacious landscaped grounds with tennis courts and swimming pools, such as Rambagh Palace in Jaipur or Umaid Bhawan in Jodhpur. Similarly appointed pleasure palaces were also built at far off game parks, where rulers could entertain their European guests at elaborate shooting parties. One of the most celebrated of these hunting palaces is Dungar Niwas at Gajner, built by Maharaja Ganga Singh of Bikaner.

The style generally chosen by the maharajas for their new palaces was a revived Rajput idiom that became popular in Rajasthan in the second half of the 19th century, surviving well into the 20th century. This architectural style exploited the Rajput love for arcaded wings and porticos, octagonal towers topped by *chhatris*, and rooftop terraces dotted with pavilions with curving *bangla* roofs. In reality, this revived manner owed much to the European enthusiasm for Rajasthan's art and craft traditions. A key figure in this regard was Colonel (later Sir) Samuel Swinton Jacob, an engineer in the British army stationed in Jaipur. In 1890, Jacob published his *Jeypore Portfolio* of detailed drawings, which drew attention to the skills of traditional builders, masons and metalsmiths, who were employed by him in many of the new palaces that he built for the maharajas. Among Jacob's most ambitious projects were Rambagh Palace in Jaipur, Umed Bhawan in Kota, and Lallgarh in Bikaner. Built in an unabashedly revived Rajput idiom, these royal complexes were carefully planned with symmetrically disposed wings, quite unlike the earlier palaces that had grown haphazardly over many years. Jacob was particularly fond of multiple porches and terraces bristling with rooftop pavilions and *chhatris*. A hallmark of his work was the fine craftsmanship of exquisitely designed sandstone *jali* screens and *bangla* vaults with exaggeratedly curved cornices.

The maharajas also employed this revived Rajput style in the civic monuments they erected in their capitals, thereby demonstrating the suitability of this idiom for different building types, not merely palaces. This idiom, no doubt, had a particular appeal because it contrasted favourably with the obviously European appearance of imported neo-Classical or neo-Gothic styles that were promoted by the British for their own official buildings. As feelings of nationalism gathered strength in the course of the 19th and 20th centuries, the choice of an appropriate architectural idiom became a subject of discussion for the maharajas. The town halls, clock towers, museums, colleges and hospitals they built in the Rajput revived manner within their cities expressed a confidence in an indigenous style as well as a civic enlightenment that was in keeping with the time. Nor were the British immune to the charms of neo-Rajput architecture, judging from the profusion of administrative buildings they erected in this same style throughout their Indian dominions, well beyond Rajasthan.

As this revivalist mode was gaining widespread popularity, many rulers in Rajasthan, as indeed elsewhere in India during this period, fell under the spell of European architecture. Neo-Classical columns, pediments, pilasters and balustrades made an appearance as part of a broader fashion for British ceremony, costume and regalia. Meanwhile, maharajas commissioned royal portraits to be executed in oil on canvas, which they proudly displayed in their darbar halls, and also ordered British-styled coats of arms. Palace interiors were filled with imported or imitation European furniture, chandeliers and mirrors. Nowhere is this better illustrated than in the Rambagh and Bissau Palaces of Jaipur, or the palace of the descendants of Rao Shekha in Shahpura, to the north of Jaipur. In fact, European decoration had already been popular in Rajasthan since the second half of the 18th century, as is obvious from the English, or perhaps Dutch, blue-and-white ceramic plates set into walls of Badi Chatur Chowk in Udaipur's City Palace and Am Khas in Juna Mahal at Dungarpur. Europeans were sometimes viewed as curiosities and became the subject of wall decoration, as may be seen in the coloured mosaic compositions in both these palaces, as well as in the murals that adorned the mansions of Shekhawati.

This fascination with Europe extended into the 20th century, by which time most maharajas in Rajasthan had enthusiastically adopted western clothes, cars and sports, let alone architectural styles. Some of the pleasure resorts, which served as fashionable retreats for the maharajas, were built in the 1920s and 1930s in the latest Modernist manner, complete with contemporary furniture and fittings ordered from London or Paris. European artists in India, such as Julius Stefan Norblin who was active in Rajasthan in the 1940s, were commissioned to adorn the interiors with murals, and even design the furniture when this could no longer be imported from London or Paris once World War II broke out. Art Deco found an enthusiastic following in Rajasthan, probably because its elegant streamlined contours and boldly sculpted imagery suited the progressive mood of many rulers at this time. The Art Deco Umaid Bhawan in Jodhpur represents the climax of the Indian penchant for European Modernism. Not only is it the grandest of all 20th-century royal residences in India, it is also a testament to the synthesis that was possible between the traditional architecture of Rajasthan and that of contemporary Europe.

FOLLOWING PAGES A full-length portrait of Saheb Bhagh Singh, a local *thakur*, at the entrance to the circular *shish mahal* in a corner tower of Bala Qila, the fortified palace in the middle of Nawalgarh, in Shekhawati.

JAIPUR

The city of Jaipur was founded in 1727 by Maharaja Sawai Jai Singh II as the new capital of the Kachhawaha kingdom, after he moved from Amber, 12 kilometres to the north. Claiming descent from Kush, son of the god Rama, the Kachhawaha rulers in north-eastern Rajasthan trace their origins back to the 12th century, when they seized the fort at Amber from local Mina tribesmen. However, it was only during the Mughal period that the Kachhawaha family rose to greatness. Raja Bharmal (1548-74) was the first Rajput ruler to forge an alliance with Akbar, to whom he offered his daughter in marriage in 1562. (She was to become the mother of Salim, the future emperor Jahangir.) This matrimonial alliance elevated the Kachhawahas to the highest position at the Mughal court, thereby promoting their careers over the next two hundred years. Both Bharmal and his son, Raja Bhagwant Das (1574-89), served Akbar with distinction in different parts of the empire, including Bihar and Bengal. The same is true of Bharmal's nephew and eventual successor, Raja Man Singh I (1589-1614), who commanded the Mughal forces with considerable success in Gujarat, Bengal and Afghanistan. In 1576, he led a punitive expedition against the neighbouring kingdom of Udaipur, which had refused to submit to Mughal authority. Man Singh was a great builder, and the imposing palace at Amber was begun under his reign. His predecessors lived in more modest residences, of which no trace survives. The next ruler of note, Mirza Raja Jai Singh I (1621-67), continued the Kachhawaha tradition of service under the Mughals. Much of his long reign was spent fighting battles and administering provinces, including the Deccan, on behalf of Shah Jahan and Aurangzeb. In 1665, he compelled Shivaji, the Maratha warrior chief who had challenged the Mughal army, to sign a treaty of capitulation.

Maharaja Sawai Jai Singh II (1700-43), the next significant ruler, was responsible for shifting the Kachhawaha headquarters from fortified Amber to a magnificently laid out city in the plains, east of the Aravalli Hills, an act that proclaimed his status as the most powerful Rajput figure of his time. Named after him, the new capital of Jaipur was built as a walled city that conformed to traditional Hindu principles of town planning, with the City Palace in the centre surrounded by a regular grid of broad streets lined with bazaars, workshops and mansions, all supplied with a reliable water system. In the royal complex was an observatory where Jai Singh could study the movement of the sun and stars, thereby predicting events and asserting symbolic control over his kingdom. Like his predecessors, Jai Singh was occupied with governing the Mughal provinces, including Agra, from where he forged an alliance with the Jats of nearby Bharatpur, thereby harnessing their martial skills to the imperial cause. As the Mughal control over Rajasthan weakened during the first half of the 18th century, Jai Singh expanded the Kachhawaha territories and developed Jaipur into a haven for bankers, merchants and jewellers. Jaipur's prosperity was sustained under Maharaja Sawai Ishwari Singh (1743-50), in spite of an incursion by the Udaipur army. The resulting turbulence did not prevent this ruler from patronizing many literary and artistic works, and making substantial additions to the City Palace. Maharaja Sawai Madho Singh I's reign (1750-67) was marred by Maratha invasions and acute rivalry with the Rathors of Jodhpur, a situation that continued into the early years of the 19th century, till Jaipur aligned itself with the East India Company. In 1818, a treaty with the British guaranteed protection to Jaipur, but security came at a cost, and a Resident was permanently posted at the Kachhawaha court.

Maharaja Sawai Ram Singh II (1835-80) was the first significant Kachhawaha ruler of the British period. His many years on the Jaipur throne are marked by loyalty to the foreign power and implementation of social and educational reforms. It was this ruler who initiated the colour washing of Jaipur's buildings, thereby earning it the sobriquet, Pink City. Similar progressive policies were sustained under Maharaja Sawai Madho Singh II (1880-1922), who pursued a programme of planned economic development. The first Jaipur Exhibition of 1883 was supervised by Samuel Swinton Jacob, who did much to promote the revival of Rajput architecture and art. Madho Singh was a staunch supporter of the British. He attended the coronation of Edward VII in 1902, travelling to London with his own supply of sacred Ganga water stored in large silver vessels, and was also present at the Delhi Darbars of 1903 and 1911. Furthermore, he played host to the Prince of Wales and Queen Mary, and also contributed troops and funds to the British effort during World War I.

The next Kachhawaha ruler, Maharaja (Sir) Sawai Man Singh II (1922-70), was an adopted relative who assumed full powers in 1931. During his reign, Jaipur continued to evolve as a progressive state, but Man Singh gained particular fame as a dashing polo player, bringing his team to England in 1933, and then as the husband of Gayatri Devi, the glamorous princess from Cooch Behar, whom he took as his third wife in 1940. After India's independence, Man Singh was honoured with the post of Rajpramukh (Head of State) for the Union of Greater Rajasthan, with Jaipur as capital. The Kachhawaha family is today represented by Brigadier Sawai Bhawani Singh, a soldier with more than twenty years of distinguished service in the Indian army.

FOLLOWING PAGES Picturesquely set in the wooded Aravalli Hills, Amber Palace was the residence of the Kachhawaha rulers prior to the foundation of City Palace in Jaipur.

LEFT Rajendra Pol, the main gateway to the second courtyard of City Palace, as viewed through the delicate arched tracery of Mubarak Mahal's balcony.

BELOW A gateway in one of the outer courtyards of the complex, with the upper pavilions of Hawa Mahal beyond.

CITY PALACE

The City Palace in Jaipur has served as the principal residence of the Kachhawaha rulers since 1727, when Maharaja Sawai Jai Singh II initiated work on it. The vast complex is contained by high walls with monumental arched gateways on three sides providing access to the broad bazaar streets of the city. The sequence of *chowks* (courtyards) inside the palace begins with the outermost precinct that accommodates Jantar Mantar, Jai Singh's personal observatory. Mubarak Mahal, a pavilion designed by Samuel Swinton Jacob, graces the frst inner courtyard. From here, Rajendra Pol, a gateway also designed by Jacob, leads to the second courtyard in the middle of which stands Sarvatobhadra, the public audience hall. Overlooking the third courtyard, Pritam Niwas Chowk, is Chandra Mahal, a lofty seven-storey wing that dominates the entire complex. This vertical stack of reception chambers and residential apartments faces north towards a grand formal garden.

ABOVE The clock tower soaring above the courtyard of Sarvatobhadra is an early-20th-century addition modelled on British civic architecture.

ABOVE RIGHT Windows set in temple-like frames have Mughal style arches painted around them, in the Sarvatobhadra courtyard.

LEFT A detail of the lotus pond mural that covers the side walls of Pritam Niwas Chowk, the third courtyard of Jaipur's City Palace.

FAR LEFT The doorways in the middle of the four walls around Pritam Niwas Chowk symbolize the different seasons. The painted rose petal design above this doorway represents winter. In the centre is a miniature carved relief of the god Shiva and his consort Parvati, above a painted sun motif.

RIGHT This embossed brass door with painted peacock feather motifs above represents summer.

LEFT A portrait of Maharaja Sawai Jai Singh II, the founder of Jaipur's City Palace, in the veranda apartment of Chandra Mahal.

RIGHT Royal portraits and swirling arabesque in the veranda apartment were painted by European artists in the 1940s.

BELOW LEFT Sukh Niwas, the double-height reception hall on the first level of Chandra Mahal at the core of Jaipur's City Palace, was refurbished in the 20th century to serve as a private dining and sitting area.

BELOW Silver hookahs and rose water sprinklers are displayed on the side tables near the sitting area in Sukh Niwas.

ABOVE RIGHT Silver objects and photographs decorate the comfortable sitting area of Sukh Niwas. Tiny peepholes in the painted windows above allowed courtly women to observe the entertainments.

ABOVE The upper levels of Chandra Mahal, the core wing of Jaipur's City Palace, are topped by a small pavilion; illuminated at night, they form the perfect backdrop to outdoor dining on the terrace below.

LEFT Exquisitely painted with blue-and-white foliate designs, Chhavi Niwas, the apartment on the fourth level of Chandra Mahal, was originally intended for private receptions.

LEFT The steeply angled staircase of Samrat Yantra, the astronomical instrument that forms the centrepiece of the Jantar Mantar observatory in the outermost courtyard of Jaipur's City Palace. The observatory was built in 1734 by Maharaja Sawai Jai Singh II.

RIGHT The curved, calibrated marble scale of Samrat Yantra is used for measuring the moving shadow of the staircase, thereby precisely determining local time.

FOLLOWING PAGES, LEFT Suraj Pol, the east gateway of City Palace, leads to one of the main bazaar streets of Jaipur. This broad, straight thoroughfare is flanked by shops and houses with pink façades.

FOLLOWING PAGES, RIGHT A detail of the whimsical façade of Hawa Mahal at the eastern periphery of City Palace. Tier upon tier of screened windows, topped by fanciful vaults, allowed courtly women to gaze down on a bustling bazaar street.

RIGHT The neo-Classical indoor swimming pool was once equipped with a diving board, and even a trapeze suspended from the ceiling for water acrobatics.

BELOW Rooftop *chhatris* at the end of a residential wing serve as lookout points with fine views of the surrounding garden.

BOTTOM The luxuriously appointed marble bathroom in the Maharani Suite has a geometric patterned floor in white marble and yellow Jaisalmer stone.

ABOVE An alcove with cane chairs by the indoor swimming pool.

FOLLOWING PAGES, LEFT The dining room is conceived as a splendid European baroque banquet hall, complete with frescoes illustrating scenes from classical mythology.

FOLLOWING PAGES, RIGHT Venetian gold glass mosaic panels with vase-and-foliage motifs enhance the sitting area in the veranda.

RAMBAGH PALACE

Located just south of Jaipur's old walled city, this palace takes its name from a garden pavilion where Maharaja Sawai Ram Singh II lived as a child for some years after 1836. The pavilion was replaced by a modest lodge in 1887 during Maharaja Sawai Madho Singh's reign, and was further expanded into a grandly scaled palace for royal guests in the early years of the 20th century, according to designs by Samuel Swinton Jacob. The central wing of the palace accommodates a reception hall and banquet room, fronted by a veranda facing a beautifully landscaped garden with pools, where peacocks can usually be seen strutting around. Maharaja Sawai Man Singh II made Rambagh his principal residence in 1925, and continued to live here after his marriage to Gayatri Devi in 1940. The palace was refurbished as a deluxe hotel in 1957, though care was taken to retain the original polo bar, banquet room, indoor pool and magnificent garden, much to the delight of present-day visitors.

BELOW The broad marble staircase in the entrance hall has balustrades of perforated *jali* screens, also in marble; the sculpted lion torsos are a replica of India's national emblem.

BOTTOM Neo-Classical fluted columns line the garden veranda of the palace.

RAJ MAHAL

Originally built in 1729 as a garden residence for Chandra Kunwar, the wife of Maharaja Sawai Jai Singh II, this palace in Jaipur was inhabited by different members of the Kachhawaha family for over a hundred years. In 1835, it was handed over to Major Stewart, the British Resident at the Kachhawaha court, after which it came to be known as the Residency. The building remained with the British until independence in 1947, and in 1959 it was occupied by Maharaja Sawai Man Singh II and Maharani Gayatri Devi who renamed it Raj Mahal. The royal couple had the palace extensively remodelled by British decorators, who adopted a restrained style that blended revived Rajput features with an elegant neo-Classicism. This somewhat hybrid idiom accorded well with the progressive architectural trends of the time. Among the most illustrious personal guests received by the royal couple were Queen Elizabeth II and Jacqueline Kennedy. Raj Mahal was converted into a small hotel in 1976.

LEFT Detail of the European-styled mirror and *chaise longue* in the enormous wood panelled Maharani Suite.

LILYPOOL

In the 1930s, Maharaja Sawai Man Singh II of Jaipur decided to transform a tennis pavilion in the garden of Rambagh into a modest palace where he could entertain private guests. On this new project he bestowed the somewhat whimsical name, Lilypool. Designed by an Austrian architect then working in India, Lilypool was conceived as a comfortable European villa with only occasional features derived from traditional Rajput architecture. In 1969, Man Singh began to refurbish Lilypool, intending it as a residence for himself and his wife, Maharani Gayatri Devi. It was smaller in size and more intimate in atmosphere than Raj Mahal, their home at this time, but no doubt equally comfortable. Sadly, he died before work was completed. Gayatri Devi moved into Lilypool in 1978, and has since made this her principal residence in Jaipur. Much of the silverware and Lalique crystal furniture that graces the interior came from Raj Mahal, but has now become an essential part of Lilypool.

LEFT The refined painted wall decoration
of Rasal Mahal on the first level is typical of
the revived Rajput style that continued to
be popular in Jaipur in the 20th century.

BELOW The *chaise longue* and mirrored
dressing table in one of the bedrooms at the
ground level are in the European manner.

NARAIN NIWAS

This palace in Jaipur, opposite Rambagh, occupies the site of the garden residence of Narain Singh, a *thakur* of the Kanota family who rose to power at the Kachhawaha court under Maharaja Sawai Ram Singh II in the second half of the 19th century. Narain Singh used the residence as a retreat from his busy administrative and court duties in Jaipur, which continued well into the 20th century. Four years after his death in 1924, his son Amar Singh rebuilt the residence as a hunting palace, since it was at the time surrounded by forest. He selected a revived Rajput idiom for the new building, which was equipped with modern facilities. Amar Singh gained renown not only as a capable administrator and sportsman, but also as a diarist who vividly recorded details of the period 1898-1942, during which he lived in Narain Niwas. The palace continued to serve as a private residence of his descendants until 1978, when Mohan Singh, the present representative of the family, transformed it into a hotel.

FOLLOWING PAGES The former darbar hall of Narain Niwas, now the principal reception area of the hotel, is divided into two parts by a brightly coloured arcade. The European-styled chairs and tables, glass cabinets and pendulum clock, all date from the period of Amar Singh.

RIGHT The high, green veranda of the palace has neo-Classical panelled doors that open into the Darbar Hall.

BELOW A figure of Hanuman, the valiant monkey god of Indian mythology, is incorporated into the elaborate wrought-iron entrance gate.

BOTTOM Neo-Classical columns, doors and windows betray a preoccupation with European styles.

DIGGI PALACE

The *thakurs* of Diggi, an estate about 40 kilometres south-west of Jaipur, were Khangarwat Rajputs, who served with distinction in the Jaipur army during the 18th and 19th centuries. Before his death in 1880, Maharaja Sawai Ram Singh II offered Sahib Pratap Singh of Diggi a royal property just south of Jaipur's walled city, and this *thakur* immediately set about establishing a garden resort, complete with stables for horses and elephants. In 1881, Pratap Singh began work on an ambitious palace on this site. He built the Diggi Palace in the revived Rajput style, but with distinct European features that were still relatively novel in Jaipur. The magnifcent Darbar Hall constitutes a detached block in the middle of the palace where Pratap Singh and his successors entertained visitors and enjoyed performances of music and dance. Similar activities still take place in the hall, since the palace is now a hotel with guests staying in a separate residential wing.

RIGHT The grandiose scale of the Darbar Hall is emphasized by transverse arches and an arcade of lobed arches at the rear, all brightly painted with floral motifs.

BELOW The library with its many bookshelves also houses a fine collection of silverware.

BOTTOM European-styled beds with carved wooden frames and inset ceramic panels furnish one of the bedrooms in the palace.

BISSAU PALACE

Established during the reign of Maharaja Sawai Jagat Singh (1803-18), Bissau Palace in the old bazaar to the west of the walled city was intended as the Jaipur home of the rawals of Bissau, an estate in Shekhawati, 170 kilometres north-east of Jaipur. The present building, however, with its heavy wooden furniture and formal oil paintings dates only from 1919. Since the then rawal of Bissau, Bishan Singh, spent most of his time with his English friends abroad, the design and construction work came under the supervision of his son, the youthful Raghubir Singh. By the time of Bishan Singh's death in 1945, the palace had fallen into disrepair, and once again it was Raghubir Singh who oversaw the renovations. Like the other city residences of the Jaipur *thakur*s, Bissau Palace testifes to the popularity of European styles and modes of living in Jaipur in the 20th century. Now established as a hotel, the palace is a showpiece of local family history and art collections.

ABOVE The sitting room has French-styled
console tables, Modernist shelves, and
full-scale oil paintings portraying Rawals
Bishan Singh (1891-1945) on the left
and Jagat Singh (1875-93) on the right.

SAMODE HAVELI

Like the *thakurs* of Diggi and Bissau, the Nathawat rawals of Samode, about 40 kilometres north of Jaipur, rose to prominence at the Kachhawaha court in the course of the 19th century. Rawal Bairi Sal of Samode was in fact the principal signatory, on behalf of Maharaja Sawai Jagat Singh, of the historic 1818 treaty that made Jaipur a protectorate of the British East India Company. Bairi Sal later became the prime minister of the Jaipur state, wielding considerable influence up until 1838. In addition to refurbishing his hereditary palace at Samode, he also erected a sumptuously appointed *haveli* inside the walls of Jaipur city that served as an urban residence. As in the palace at Samode itself, Samode Haveli is ornamented with exquisite murals and dense patterns of inlaid mirror work, much of it added by Rawal Sheo Singh, Bairi Sal's son. Their descendants still own the property, which has now been converted into a charming hotel.

ABOVE Light streaming in through the windows illuminates a cushioned sitting area with a traditional writing desk (in the same apartment as shown on the extreme left).

JAL MAHAL & JAIGARH

About halfway along the Jaipur-Amber road is Man Sagar, an artifcial lake created in the early 17th century by Raja Man Singh I of Amber. In the middle of the lake stands the gracious island pavilion of Jal Mahal, built by Maharaja Sawai Pratap Singh (1778-1803), who intended it as a pleasure resort and shooting box to hunt waterfowl. Its *bangla*-topped pavilions and corner *chhatris* overlook the lake.

The road proceeds to the mountain pass in the Aravalli Hills, guarded by the great Amber Palace established by Man Singh. The citadel of Jaigarh, crowning the ridge immediately above the palace, was founded by the same maharaja, but named after Sawai Jai Singh II who completed its walls, towers and pavilions in 1725. While the great fortifed enclosure of Jaigarh at the top of the hill and the cannons that defended the palace below can still be seen, nothing has ever been found of Man Singh's legendary treasure looted from various campaigns and supposedly buried in Jaigarh.

LEFT When the waters of Man Sagar are high, the island pavilion of Jal Mahal can only be reached by boat. Its incomparable location made it ideal for lakeside picnics.

RIGHT The arcades surrounding the terrace of Jaigarh look down onto a watchtower that guards the lower walls.

ABOVE The impressive ramparts of
Amber Palace are reflected in the still
waters of Maota Lake.

AMBER PALACE

Although Amber was the principal residence of the Kachhawaha rulers from the 12th century until the move to Jaipur in 1727, the magnifcent palace here dates only from the very end of the 16th century, during the reign of Raja Man Singh I. The strongly fortifed complex is built on a steep hill overlooking Maota Lake, beside which runs the old highway to Delhi. The palace consists of a string of courtyards, audience halls and private apartments on different levels, beginning with Jaleb Chowk where troops and animals could assemble, and ending with the original residence of Man Singh, later converted into a *zenana*. The intermediate courts with the Diwan-i Am and the residential apartments, known variously as Sukh, Jai and Jas Mandirs, were all added by Mirza Raja Jai Singh I in the early 17th century. Built in a strikingly pure Mughal style and decorated in the fnest Mughal manner, the apartments proclaim the close connections between the Kachhawahas and the Mughal emperors.

FOLLOWING PAGES, LEFT A painted detail over the arched gateway of Ganesh Pol depicts the elephant-headed god Ganesha, after whom the gateway is named.

FOLLOWING PAGES, RIGHT Arcades in the private audience hall in the second courtyard of Amber Palace are covered in polished plaster imitating white marble.

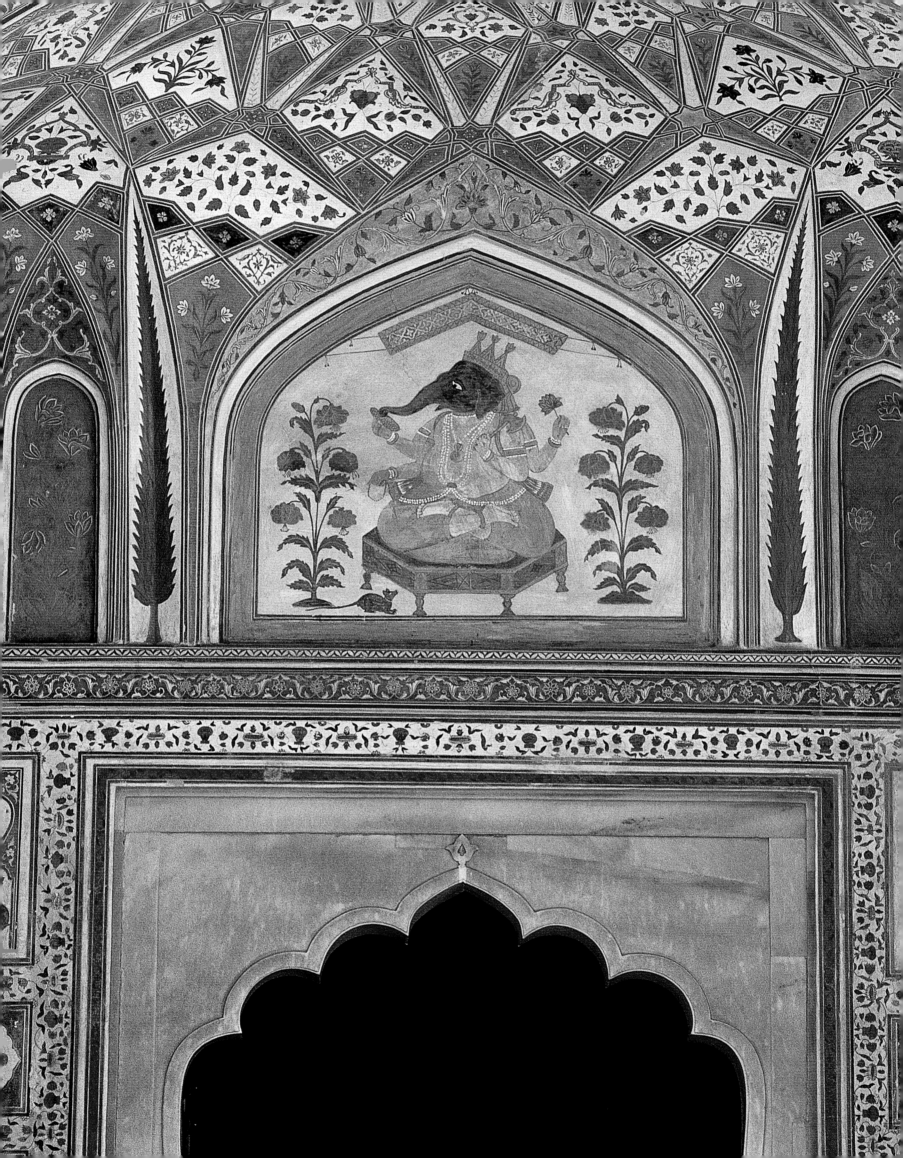

ABOVE The walls lining the veranda of the *shish mahal* in Jai Mandir are divided into panels with opulent relief designs and inlaid mirror work.

RIGHT The dazzling ceiling of the *shish mahal* in Jai Mandir at Amber Palace is divided into innumerable curving facets coated with tiny pieces of mirror; the walls beneath are enhanced by vase-shaped niches and relief panels.

BELOW The palace with its succession
of walled courtyards is tucked away in
the rugged Aravalli Hills.

SAMODE PALACE

The palace at Samode, 40 kilometres
north of Jaipur, is the residence of the
Nathawat rawals, a family of *thakurs* that
served under the Jaipur rulers, but trace
their origins back to the period when
Amber was the Kachhawaha capital.
The complex at Samode dates mainly
from the period of Rawals Bairi Sal and
Sheo Singh, prime ministers under
Maharajas Sawai Jai Singh III (1819-35)
and his successor Sawai Ram Singh II.
The two rawals are credited with building
the audience hall in the middle of
Samode Palace, as well as the private
apartments at the rear, all of which open
off three courtyards arranged in a linear
succession. The extravagant murals
and mirror work gracing the interiors
have been meticulously renewed.
The property, still in the possession
of the Nathawat family, now functions
as a hotel. Together with the spacious
gardens a short distance away, the
palace attained international fame when
it appeared in the television version of
The Far Pavilions.

FOLLOWING PAGES, LEFT A seemingly
infinite perspective of the upper level of the
zenana in Samode Palace, as seen through
a sequence of profusely ornamented windows.

FOLLOWING PAGES, RIGHT A shuttered
window surrounded by painted panels in
the upper level of the Darbar Hall.

ABOVE The corner watchtower stands vigil
over the road ascending to the arched gateway
of the outermost courtyard.

Dancing maidens grace the walls (*left*), and female musicians the arches (*right*) of Sultan Mahal, the apartment that opens onto the first inner courtyard of Samode Palace.

RIGHT A cushioned seat is positioned in front of the central arched recess in Sultan Mahal, with courtly scenes painted on the side walls.

FOLLOWING PAGES The principal reception room in the *zenana* of Samode Palace is adorned with murals and mirrored pieces to create a gleaming *shish mahal*.

BELOW A neo-Classical arcade with slender
columns is skirted by a neatly manicured
lawn that slopes down to Ramgarh Lake.

RAMGARH LODGE

Located 35 kilometres north-east of
Jaipur, in the wooded ranges of Alwar
Hills, this lodge stands on the northern
shore of the extensive Ramgarh Lake.
The lake was dammed in 1902 by
Maharaja Sawai Madho Singh II to serve
as the principal water supply for Jaipur
city. Since the lake attracted large fbcks
of waterfowl in winter, the surrounding
area was developed into a game park for
the hunting activities of the Jaipur royal
family. In 1937, Sawai Man Singh II
erected a small palace with sleek Art
Deco interiors to serve as a shooting
lodge for the maharaja and his visitors.
It was here that Man Singh and Gayatri
Devi welcomed guests on the occasion
of their marriage three years later. The
principal reception room of Ramgarh
Lodge opens onto an arcaded veranda
leading to the garden. It is surrounded
by a dining hall, bar and billiard room,
all well stocked with memorabilia of past
hunting expeditions undertaken by the
Jaipur maharajas elsewhere in India as
well as in East Africa.

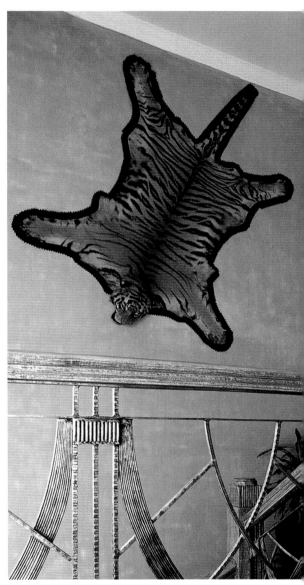

ABOVE LEFT A fierce lion and somewhat comical bear appear to guard the glass door leading to the bar.

ABOVE An Art Deco metal-and-glass lamp illuminates a translucent photograph of Maharani Gayatri Devi.

ABOVE RIGHT The elegant Art Deco metal balustrade on a staircase landing, with a tiger skin splayed out on the wall above.

BELOW The small, picturesque Jogi Mahal, deep within the national park, with the impregnable battlements of the fort looming above.

RANTHAMBHOR

Once the private tiger reserve of the Jaipur maharajas, Ranthambhor is now a national park under the Project Tiger scheme. It lies 180 kilometres south-east of Jaipur. The fort on top of the high cliff within the park's 400 square kilometres dates back to the 13th century, when it was occupied by the Chauhan Rajputs; no palace survives from this early period. Jogi Mahal, the small sandstone pavilion beside a lake at the foot of the fort, was only erected in the 1930s by Sawai Man Singh II as a temporary shelter for day visitors to the park. The maharaja's hunting parties were accommodated a short distance outside the park in Sawai Madhopur Lodge. This residence was adorned with exuberant Art Deco interiors, many of them with exotic jungle themes. Among the distinguished guests was Queen Elizabeth II, who stayed here in 1962. The lodge has been recently converted into a hotel, attracting wildlife enthusiasts as well as those seeking peace and quiet in a forested setting.

RIGHT A tigerskin bench beneath a mural showing elephants in the alcove of the bar in Sawai Madhopur Lodge.

SHEKHAWATI

Wedged between the powerful kingdoms of Jaipur and Bikaner in northern Rajasthan, the somewhat arid region of Shekhawati to the west of the Aravalli Hills was long divided into a number of small estates, each with its own line of rulers. For this reason, it never achieved autonomy as an independent kingdom. In the 15th century, Shekhawati came under the sway of the Kachhawahas of Amber, who themselves were subservient to the Delhi sultans. It was during this period that Rao Shekha (1433-88) of Shahpura, which is just over 50 kilometres north of Amber, rose to prominence as a fearless military figure. Taking the aid of some discontented Muslim mercenaries who were at the time returning to their homeland in Afghanistan from Gujarat, Shekha challenged the power of the Amber rulers. Though in the end he was unable to establish a truly autonomous state, he gave his name to a number of related warrior families that came to be known as Shekhawats. Their true history begins only at the end of the 16th century when the Mughal emperor, Akbar, awarded lands to several of his loyal Shekhawat followers. Among them was Raisalji, to whom he granted the estate of Khandela, about 80 kilometres north-west of Amber. Akbar also bestowed on him the title of 'raja' in return for his courage in protecting the emperor's person. By the turn of the 17th century, Raisalji's sons, Bhojraj and Tirmul, managed to forge a small kingdom centred on Khandela, while maintaining good relations with their more powerful neighbours, the Kachhawahas.

The successors of Bhojraj and Tirmul brought much of the territory around Khandela under their control. In 1730, Shardul Singh, a descendant of Bhojraj, seized Jhunjhunun, a town about 65 kilometres north of Khandela, which had been controlled by a local nawab. The following year, Shardul Singh allied himself with one of Tirmul's successors, and together they evicted the nawab of Fatehpur, another important town in the region. Since Jhunjhunun was the largest and richest of these holdings, the fate of Shardul Singh and his heirs is central to Shekhawati's history. Tradition required that Shardul Singh divide his lands between his five sons. Accordingly, one of his sons, Nawal Singh, established Nawalgarh and Mandawa in 1737 and 1756 respectively; another son, Keshri Singh, founded Bissau in 1746 and Dundlod in 1750. The two brothers developed these villages into substantial fortified towns, each of which became headquarters of a small but independent estate governed by a line of Shekhawat *thakurs*.

After Maharaja Sawai Jai Singh II moved the Kachhawaha capital to Jaipur in 1727, he and his heirs successfully imposed their sovereignty on the Shekhawats, reducing them to the status of *thakurs* (landed nobles). Even so, these figures managed to retain their hereditary properties, which they ruled in a more or less self-governing fashion. There was, however, always the danger of dividing the lands into ever-smaller holdings between competing brothers. In the course of the 18th century, the Shekhawat *thakurs* sought service in the Jaipur army, where they earned renown as valiant warriors, assisting the Kachhawahas in their struggles against the Marathas and Jats. Together with their military retinues, they became famous for their skill as horsemen, and formed the backbone of the Jaipur cavalry.

In spite of their employment in the Jaipur army, many Shekhawat *thakurs* attempted to supplement the meagre earnings from their decreased estates by resorting to banditry. Shyam Singh (1787-1833) of Bissau, who maintained a private force, including two French mercenaries, and several of his contemporaries became notorious for raiding their neighbours and attacking trade caravans that passed across the region. In 1835, in a bid to restore law and order, the British East India Company recommended the formation of the Shekhawati Brigade, an army of local troops that was successful in curbing the excesses of these *thakurs*. After some measure of order was restored, many of the more important Shekhawat *thakurs* moved to Jaipur with their families, where they rose to prominence as nobles at the Kachhawaha court and built their *havelis*, or city mansions. Following the example of the Jaipur maharajas, the Shekhawats also championed British causes, sending troops to support them during the uprising of 1857.

In addition to their military and administrative careers, the Shekhawat *thakurs* were also concerned about boosting their fortunes. In the early 19th century, the wiser *thakurs* invited merchants from Jaipur and its environs to settle on their estates, where many of them prospered by engaging in business with the caravans that traversed the Shekhawati region laden with goods. However, with the decline in the caravan trade later in the 19th century due to the introduction of the railways by the British, many of these merchant families left Shekhawati to seek their fortunes in the newly flourishing port cities of Calcutta and Bombay. Here they came to be known collectively as Marwaris, even though they did not actually come from Marwar (Jodhpur). This, then, is the origin of the Birlas, Goenkas and Poddars, whose industrial and commercial enterprises now encompass the whole of India. Most of these Marwari families still maintain their ancestral homes in the various towns of Shekhawati. As for the descendants of the *thakurs* who had originally persuaded these merchants to settle in Shekhawati, they divide their time between their inherited country estates and more comfortable city mansions in Jaipur.

PRECEDING PAGES A canon still guards the arched gateway to the restored inner courtyard of Castle Mandawa.

BELOW Rounded arches and columns distinguish this bedroom at the upper level of Castle Mandawa.

CASTLE MANDAWA
& MANDAWA HAVELI

Mandawa, a town 25 kilometres south-west of Jhunjhunun, and one of the largest estates of Shekhawati, traces its history to Thakur Nawal Singh who founded it in 1756. In the same year, he initiated work on a quadrangular fortifed building in the middle of Mandawa. Under his grandsons, Padara Singh (1775-80) and Gyan Singh (1780-1824), this was expanded into a spacious and comfortable residence with accommodation arranged around a sequence of courtyards. Fine murals adorn the exterior and interior of the palace, which has now taken on new life as Castle Mandawa Hotel.

Murals are also found on the façade of the many fne mansions erected in Mandawa in the course of the 19th century. Mandawa Haveli, a typical example dating from 1890, is associated with the Sarafs, one of the leading merchant families of the town. This mansion with original paintings has now been converted into a hotel.

RIGHT Maidens in different costumes and busts of armed warriors animate the courtyard of Gopesh Suite in Mandawa Haveli.

BELOW The doorway leading into the second courtyard of Poddar Haveli and the arched niches to one side are covered with murals.

PODDAR & BHAGAT HAVELIS, NAWALGARH

Nawalgarh, 38 kilometres south of Jhunjhunun, is one of the oldest towns in Shekhawati, having been founded by Thakur Nawal Singh in 1737. That Nawalgarh attained considerable prosperity in the course of the 19th and early 20th centuries is demonstrated by the many fne *havelis* belonging to the Marwari merchant families, which line the narrow streets of the town. The mansion built by Anandi Lal Poddar at the turn of the 20th century is remarkable for its lively murals showing mythological and secular scenes, including trains and cars. The building now houses a school that bears the name of its founder.

Another notable mansion in Nawalgarh dating from the same period is Bhagat Haveli. This has two courts separated by a double-height reception room adorned with murals, both inside and out, at the upper level. Many of these paintings depict Europeans, who must have been of considerable fascination for the inhabitants of the *haveli*.

ABOVE The reception room in Bhagat Haveli
has curious wall paintings of Europeans.

DUNDLOD CASTLE

This building started out as a small fort established in 1750 by Thakur Keshri Singh to accommodate his private contingent of soldiers. Located in the town of Dundlod, 24 kilometres south of Jhunjhunun, the fort served as a refuge for his descendant, Sheo Singh, who fled Jhunjhunun in 1809, after his father and brother were murdered by Shyam Singh of Bissau, one of the most notorious Shekhawat *thakurs* of the era. It was Sheo Singh who was responsible for converting the fort into a palatial residence worthy of the Dundlod *thakurs*, one of the most powerful families of Shekhawati. Much of the present complex, however, including the impressive Darbar Hall, dates from about 1840. The residence also houses a significant library of books and manuscripts. This collection belongs to Rawal Harnath Singh (1905-76), who attained particular renown as a scholar. In 1972, he had a portion of the fort converted into a hotel, naming it Dundlod Castle.

LEFT Warm ochre tones enliven the grand Darbar Hall with its lofty transverse arcade. Smaller, more intimate sitting areas open off the central space.

BELOW LEFT Looking through the colonnade and across the garden towards the imposing multi-storey gateway.

BOTTOM LEFT This ceiling painting in the reception room depicts the sun god, Surya, riding in a chariot drawn by seven horses, and surrounded by cherubic musicians.

BELOW While the wooden furniture in the reception room is modelled on European Modernist prototypes, the wall tiles were imported from England.

PIRAMAL HAVELI, BAGAR

This mansion is situated in the small
town of Bagar, 15 kilometres north-east
of Jhunjhunun. Bagar was once the
headquarters of the Nagad Pathans from
1456 till India's independence in 1947.
As elsewhere in Shekhawati, this town
was settled by enterprising merchants
in the course of the 19th century. The
wealthiest of these fgures was Seth
Piramal Chaturbhuj Makharia, who lived
from 1892 to1958, and made a fortune
in Bombay trading in cotton, opium and
silver. In 1928, he built Piramal Haveli,
a spacious residence named after him.
It was designed in an obvious European
manner with an elegant colonnaded
veranda lining a formal garden on three
sides. The airy sitting room that opens
off one of the veranda wings is
distinguished by its wooden furniture,
colourful, tiled wall panels and curiously
painted ceiling. The garden is dominated
by a monumental multi-storey gateway
that leads to the *haveli* from the street.
It was erected for the visit of Maharaja
Sawai Man Singh II of Jaipur in 1928.

RIGHT One of the angels painted on
the ceiling of the reception room wears
a conventional Indian sari and jewelled
crown, but has European-styled wings.

BELOW LEFT Painted panels bordered with foliate bands adorn a corner of the darbar hall. A portrait of Rao Pratap Singh of Shahpura rests against the wall.

BELOW An earlier portrait of Rao Pratap Singh in royal costume in the darbar hall.

BOTTOM The darbar hall is furnished with European-styled wooden furniture.

SHAHPURA

The town of Shahpura, 65 kilometres north of Jaipur on the Delhi highway, is associated with Rao Shekha. This celebrated 15th-century warrior gave his name to the Shekhawati region west of the Aravalli Hills, some distance from Shahpura. Though subordinate to the Jaipur maharajas, the Shahpura rulers were able to found a small chiefship in 1629. Their fort in the middle of the town stands to this day. As for the palace surrounded by a vast orchard on the edge of the town, this dates only from 1825, being the work of Rao Hanuwant Singh. As with the palaces of other *thakurs* who maintained close links with the Kachhawahas, this example is built in a revived Rajput style, nowhere better demonstrated than in the majestically proportioned darbar hall added to the complex in 1876, and known after its founder as Hanuwant Niwas. The hall stands in the middle of a huge garden, separate from the residential wing, part of which has now been converted into a hotel known as Shahpura Garden.

RIGHT The darbar hall is dominated by an imposing Belgian crystal chandelier. Among the oil portraits on the rear wall are those of Kunwar Kalyan Singh of Shahpura and Maharaja Sawai Madho Singh II of Jaipur.

ALWAR & BHARATPUR

The small forested kingdom of Alwar in eastern Rajasthan was established by Pratap Singh (1753-91), who belonged to the Lalawat Naruka clan of Rajputs. A courageous soldier, Pratap Singh earned renown in the Jaipur army for defending the fort at Ranthambhor when it was besieged by the Marathas in 1757, and aiding the Kachhawahas in their struggle against the Jat warriors in the battle of Maonda in 1767. For these acts of bravery he was rewarded with several estates to the east of the Jaipur kingdom that came to form the core of the Alwar state. By 1775, Pratap Singh had succeeded in establishing his independence by forcing the Jats to surrender the fort at Alwar, which thereupon became the headquarters of his newly founded state. He was succeeded by his adopted son, Maharaja Bakhtawar Singh (1791-1815), who collaborated with Lord Lake, commander of the East India Company forces, in the British campaign of 1803 against the Marathas. He was duly rewarded with grants of lands, thereby further augmenting the Alwar kingdom. Yet, Bakhtawar Singh remained dissatisfied, and in 1812 he attempted to occupy several forts belonging to Jaipur before being evicted by the British. The years after Bakhtawar Singh's death witnessed a succession struggle that ended only when Maharaja Vinay Singh (1826-57), his adopted nephew, was installed on the Alwar throne.

During the reign of the next ruler, Maharaja Sheodan Singh (1857-62), the Alwar kingdom plunged into chaos and bankruptcy. A council of ministers was appointed by the British Resident to replace his authority, and it remained in power until the advent of Maharaja Mangal Singh in 1874. Mangal Singh's rule, which lasted until 1892, was closely supervised by the British, with the result that some measure of peace and prosperity was restored. His successor and only son, Maharaja Jai Singh (1903-33), was an eccentric personality who gained notoriety for his love of brocaded costumes, European cars, hunting expeditions and handsome male retainers. His good looks and charm were as legendary as his unexpected fits of temper and cruelty. Jai Singh was an enthusiastic supporter of the Indian national movement, but he also overtaxed his subjects, thereby providing the British with an excuse to depose him. His last years were spent in exile in Paris. Jai Singh had no issue, and in 1937 the Alwar kingdom was inherited by a distant relative, Maharaja Tej Singh, who is the current representative of the Alwar royal family.

A little more than 100 kilometres south-east of Alwar, in the eastern extremity of Rajasthan, is Bharatpur, the older of the two Jat kingdoms in Rajasthan, the other being that of Dholpur. The Jats are the only Hindu rulers in Rajasthan who are not

Rajputs and who do not intermarry with the other royal families of the region. They claim descent from the Jadons of Bayana, a fortified town 45 kilometres south-west of Bharatpur, who earned a reputation for plunder after being dispossessed by the Delhi sultans in the 15th century. One of the first Jats to attain notoriety was Bhajja Singh (1688-95), who was killed by Aurangzeb's troops for harassing the Mughal camp. In retaliation, Bhajja's son, Chudaman Singh (1695-1721), so ravaged this part of India that the roads to Delhi and Agra were closed for some years. Farrukh Siyar, the then Mughal emperor, tried to placate this figure by granting him titles and lands in 1714. But this ruse was only partly successful, and Chudaman Singh's nephew, Badan Singh, was able to proclaim himself raja of Dig in 1722, an act that marked the foundation of the first Jat kingdom of Rajasthan.

Though he remained on the throne up to 1756, Badan Singh left the administration of his territories to his capable son, Suraj Mal, who ruled till 1763. It was Suraj Mal who captured the fort of Lohagarh at Bharatpur, 32 kilometres south of Dig, making it the new capital of his kingdom. He also marshalled the various Jat chiefs of eastern Rajasthan and central India into a powerful confederacy and raided Delhi in 1753 to plunder the Mughal treasury. In the following year, Suraj Mal defeated the Maratha forces, and in 1761 he captured Agra. It was at the Red Fort in Agra that his son, Maharaja Jawahar Singh (1763-82), temporarily established the Jat headquarters. After Jawahar Singh's defeat in the battle of Maonda in 1767, the power of the Jats declined and the confederacy disintegrated. In 1803, Maharaja Ranjit Singh (1782-1805) assisted Lord Lake in wresting Agra from the Maratha forces. Yet, the very next year he shifted his loyalties to the Marathas, permitting their troops to take refuge in the fort at Dig. The British stormed Dig, forcing the Marathas to retreat to Lohagarh. This too was besieged but never taken, and the British suffered huge losses. Thereupon, they negotiated a settlement with Ranjit Singh, by which he retained his kingdom after paying a heavy indemnity.

From this time onwards, the British kept a close eye on Bharatpur, even invading the kingdom in 1825 on the pretext of safely installing the next maharaja, Balwant Singh (1826-53), on the throne. Thereafter, the Resident became a permanent feature at Bharatpur, persuading maharajas such as Jaswant Singh (1853-92) and Kishan Singh (1900-29) to adopt progressive policies. Under Maharaja Sawai Brijendra Singh, the state was merged into modern Rajasthan in 1949. The current representative of the Bharatpur line is Vishvendra Singh.

FOLLOWING PAGES Perched above the waters of Vijay Sagar, the sprawling complex of Vijay Mandir was built by Maharaja Jai Singh of Alwar.

VINAY VILAS

Vinay Vilas, the city palace of Alwar, dates back to 1793, during the reign of Maharaja Bakhtawar Singh. It was enlarged on a number of occasions in the 19th century, most notably by Maharaja Vinay Singh, after whom the complex is named. Located beneath a precipitous hill crowned by the battlements of Bala Qila, Vinay Vilas is constructed around a central Darbar Hall that opens onto a courtyard flanked symmetrically by residential apartments. The *zenana* is located in a separate wing with its own entrance to one side. No longer used as a royal residence, the palace has been partly converted into a museum that houses a rich collection of manuscripts, miniature paintings, arms and royal regalia; the remainder of the complex accommodates government offices. The memorial *chhatri* of Bakhtawar Singh and his wife Rani Musi, who ritually immolated herself after her husband's death in 1815, stands on the edge of a grand stepped tank next to the palace.

BELOW Palace pavilions overlook the stepped tank with its octagonal towers.

LEFT Three levels of private apartments, topped by multiple *bangla* roofs, rise above the arched entrance to Zenana Mahal.

101

LEFT The gilded marble throne inside the Darbar Hall of Alwar's Vinay Vilas sits in a Mughal-styled alcove with an ornamental *bangla* vault.

RIGHT The white marble memorial *chhatri* of Bakhtawar Singh next to Vinay Vilas has a central chamber with painted designs and relief panels portraying scenes from the life of Krishna.

BELOW The domed circular chamber
crowning the watchtower of Vijay Mandir
overlooks Vijay Sagar. Staircase shafts project
on four sides of the tower.

KESROLI FORT
& VIJAY MANDIR

Dating back to the 14th century, Kesroli
Fort lies 12 kilometres north-east of
Alwar. Its impressive ramparts rise more
than 50 metres above the surrounding
countryside. The hotel concealed within
its walls occupies the former residence
of Thakur Ranawat Bhawani Singh,
a noble who attained prominence at
the Alwar court during the reign of
Maharaja Jai Singh (1903-33). The fort is
reinforced with massive circular bastions,
and the small openings are for soldiers
to train their guns.

Standing in a once-landscaped
garden near the waters of Vijay Sagar,
the vast palace of Vijay Mandir, about
10 kilometres north of Alwar, was a
personal project of Jai Singh. Throughout
the 1920s, he indulged his love of
building by adding residential wings,
courtyards, rooftops pavilions, and
fanciful domes and towers. The result
was an expansive yet picturesque folly
with more than a hundred rooms. It now
stands abandoned and forlorn.

LEFT The outer walls of Kesroli Fort, rising
over yellow fields of mustard, present a
formidable exterior. The palace within is now
converted into a hotel.

LOHAGARH

Lohagarh, or Iron Fort, served as the headquarters of the Jat kingdom of Bharatpur from the middle of the 18th century onwards. The stone-lined, circular ramparts of the fort hide from view the graceful Mughal-styled palace within. The ceremonial and residential core of the palace consists of three pavilions with arcaded verandas and occasional *bangla* vaults arranged around a pleasure garden. The oldest of these pavilions is Badan Mahal, built by Badan Singh, the first of the Bharatpur rulers. Another pavilion, Khas Mahal, added by Maharaja Balwant Singh towards the middle of the 19th century, served as the royal residence. In addition to the usual reception rooms and private chambers, Khas Mahal was also furnished with an elaborate *hammam* (steam bath). The outstanding craftsmanship of the interiors, especially the *hammam*, testifes to the wealth of the Bharatpur rulers and their desire to emulate the splendour of Mughal royal architecture.

LEFT In Badan Mahal, elegant sculpted columns with foliate bases and capitals imitate those in Mughal royal complexes.

RIGHT The central chamber of the *hammam* in Khas Mahal is roofed by a painted dome with a hole for steam to escape. The floor is decorated with inlaid polychrome stonework.

LEFT The side chamber of the *hammam* in Khas Mahal, at Bharatpur's Lohagarh, employs elegant arcades with Mughal-styled fluted columns and lobed arches. The cistern in the floor held water for bathers.

MOTI MAHAL

In the early years of the 20th century, Maharaja Kishan Singh shifted the residence of the Jat rulers of Bharatpur from Lohagarh to Moti Mahal, on the outskirts of the city. Specially designed to suit his own eclectic taste, the new palace was built in a combination of revived Rajput and Mughal styles, executed in fnely worked, dark yellow sandstone. The numerous turrets and miniature *bangla* vaults that surmount the arcades running around the palace lend a somewhat fanciful appearance to the exterior. The outstanding workmanship of the relief ornamentation and perforated *jali* screens confrms the aesthetic taste of Kishan Singh. Nowhere is this more apparent than in the graceful arcaded loggia that serves as the entrance porch to the formal apartments of the palace. Beyond lies the main reception hall, with crystal chandeliers and a chequerboard, black-and-white marble fbor, as well as a curious collection of stuffed animal trophies from local hunting expeditions.

LEFT An exquisitely crafted *jali* screen with vase-and-foliage design in the main entrance porch of Moti Mahal.

BELOW The loggia of the entrance porch employs arcades with pointed arches rising from sculpted lotus buds; the spandrels are filled with delicately carved foliation.

BELOW The elegantly arcaded Gopal Bhawan, the principal apartment of Dig Palace, and the identical Bhadon and Savan Bhawans on either side, are mirrored in the tranquil waters of Gopal Sagar.

DIG PALACE

Badan Singh selected Dig in eastern
Rajasthan as the headquarters of Jat
power in 1722; by about 1730 he began
fortifying the town with mud walls and
building a small garden palace outside
the ramparts. A few years later, his son
Suraj Mal converted this palace into
an extensive resort with two large
rectangular reservoirs, Gopal Sagar and
Rup Sagar, connected by a Mughal-
inspired, four-square garden. The garden
was provided with water channels and
fountains equipped with an ingenious
device that permitted different coloured
sprays to mingle, creating a vibrant
display. The palace itself consisted
of a number of detached, gracefully
designed pavilions that faced the garden
and sometimes also overlooked the
reservoirs. Though the capital of the
Jat rulers in this part of Rajasthan was
eventually moved to Bharatpur, 32
kilometres to the south, Dig continued to
serve as a royal resort. In fact, it was
only completed at the end of the 18th
century by Maharaja Jawahar Singh.

RIGHT Bhadon Bhawan consists of a small
bangla pavilion elevated on an arcade
projecting over the water.

FOLLOWING PAGES The spacious, arcaded
veranda of Suraj Bhawan gives onto a broad
terrace leading to the formal garden in
the middle of Dig Palace.

LEFT The swing sofa in the sitting area at the ground level of Gopal Bhawan in Dig Palace was once affixed to the perforated iron frame, cast in Glasgow.

RIGHT European-styled sofas and chairs in the spacious, arcaded sitting area of Gopal Bhawan.

BELOW RIGHT The low horseshoe-shaped dining table, carved out of marble in Gopal Bhawan, has an open-ended central section for retainers to serve food to seated guests.

BELOW The curving veranda at the upper level leads to private apartments. Its floor is composed of tile mosaic.

BELOW RIGHT Coloured ceramic tiles cover the floor and walls of this bathroom in a guest suite. Like the tiles, the tub and shower attachment were imported from England.

CITY PALACE, DHOLPUR

Dholpur served as the capital of a small Jat state in the extreme east of Rajasthan, about 65 kilometres southeast of Bharatpur. This state came into existence only in 1805 as a result of a treaty between the British and the Marathas. Maharaja Rana Kirat Singh was the frst of the Dholpur rulers, and he is credited with establishing the palace on the edge of the town. The refned neo-Classical style of its exterior and principal reception room is obviously derived from British practice, but is found nowhere else in Rajasthan. The interior of City Palace was largely remodelled by one of Kirat Singh's descendants, Maharaja Rana Udai Bhan Singh (1911-47). He was responsible for introducing the boldly patterned English tiles dating from the 1920s that almost entirely cloak the fbors and walls of the private sitting rooms, bedrooms and bathrooms. Well maintained over the years, City Palace remains the property of Hemant Singh, the present representative of the Dholpur royal family.

LEFT The supremely elegant reception room has a semicircular alcove framed by Ionic pillars, and relieved by pedimented doors and a gilded half-dome.

UDAIPUR

Mewar, the kingdom of Udaipur in southern Rajasthan, is the realm of the Sisodias, a line of rulers that has always considered itself the premier Rajput dynasty, assuming the superior title of 'rana' rather than 'raja'. Much of their prestige is derived from their valiant struggles against the sultans of the neighbouring Delhi and Malwa kingdoms in the 14th and 15th centuries, and their unwillingness to submit to the Mughals in later times. Though the Sisodias were eventually suppressed by the British in the course of the 19th century, they never relinquished their fierce spirit of independence.

The Sisodias claim descent from no less than the sun itself, hence the solar motif that serves as their family emblem. The first of the line is generally considered to be the 8th-century warrior, Bapa Rawal of the Guhilot clan, who established himself at Chittaurgarh (Chittor), the formidable hill fortress that was to serve as the Sisodia capital until 1568. One of the earliest Sisodias for whom firm historical evidence is available is Rawal Ratan Singh (1303-26). In 1303, he mounted a spirited defence of Chittaurgarh in the face of an attack from the Delhi sultans. Though he had to relinquish Chittaurgarh to the invaders, the citadel was reoccupied soon after by his son, Hamir Singh (1326-64). Under Hamir Singh and his successors, Mewar enjoyed a period of comparative stability, during which the Sisodias were able to expand their territories to the north and east. The most prominent figure of this era is Rana Kumbha (1433-68), who is credited with building the stone ramparts at Chittaurgarh, as well as various structures within this fortress, including the remarkable tower of Vijaya Stambha that commemorated his victory over the Malwa sultan in 1440. A later figure of the Sisodia line, Rana Sanga (1509-28), was also successful in battle, defeating the combined armies of Delhi and Malwa. However, one of his descendants Rana Vikramaditya (1531-36), succumbed to an attack on Chittaurgarh by Bahadur Shah of Gujarat in 1535, during which artillery was used for the first time in Rajasthan. In spite of the devastating effect of the cannons used on this occasion, Vikramaditya recovered Chittaurgarh within a few weeks.

In the following years, the Mughals posed a more serious threat to the Sisodias. It was Akbar, the first eminent Mughal ruler, who dealt the decisive blow to Chittaurgarh in the siege of 1568, after which the fortress was abandoned. When the Mughal invaders stormed the ramparts, they found the palaces deserted, and the temples engulfed in the smoke of the sacrificial pyres on which the families of the Sisodia warriors had immolated themselves. However, Rana Udai Singh (1537-72), who assumed the throne as an infant, had already shifted the principal Sisodia headquarters nine years earlier to a newly founded capital, named Udaipur after him. This was situated on the edge of an artificial lake in a sheltered valley of the Aravalli Hills, 115 kilometres west of Chittaurgarh, at a further distance from the Mughals. In spite of the obvious superiority of the Mughal army, Mewar remained hostile towards Akbar, with the result that in 1576 the emperor once again ordered an invasion of the Sisodia territories. The Mughal forces occupied both Udaipur and Chittaurgarh under their Rajput commander, Man Singh of Amber, but were eventually expelled by Rana Pratap Singh (1572-97). Difficulties with Mughals persisted until 1614, when Mewar resistance was finally worn down and Rana Amar Singh I (1597-1616) had to formally acknowledge Mughal superiority. In consequence, the Sisodia domains were left in peace to prosper once again, especially under Rana Jagat Singh I (1628-52). Relations with the Mughals now took on a more positive aspect, and it was to Udaipur that Prince Khurram, the future emperor Shah Jahan, fled in 1627-28 after an unsuccessful rebellion against his father Jahangir. The peace with the Mughals, however, was short-lived and the situation deteriorated once again under Aurangzeb, especially when the emperor mounted an invasion in 1681. Fortunately for Mewar, the Mughal forces were repelled by Rana Raj Singh I (1652-80).

As the Mughal threat declined after Aurangzeb's death in 1707, it was replaced by that of the Maratha troops who repeatedly raided Mewar demanding tribute. Rana Sangram Singh (1710-34) and his successors mostly withstood these assaults, but the kingdom was seriously weakened and its treasury depleted. During the fifty-year-long reign of Bhim Singh (1778-1828), who adopted the title of 'maharana', the Maratha threat was eventually extinguished, largely due to the efforts of the East India Company. However, the Rajput power was compromised, and the British began to intervene in local affairs. In 1818, they compelled Bhim Singh to sign a treaty of compliance. Thereafter, a British Resident was posted at the Udaipur court, the first being Colonel James Tod. Due to the cessation of wars, the fortunes of Mewar began to rise once again. Maharana Fateh Singh (1884-1929), the outstanding figure of the British period, was responsible for introducing enlightened reforms and initiating public works. Though he remained aloof from the British, Fateh Singh was awarded a nineteen-gun salute, the highest for any Rajput sovereign. Maharana Bhupal Singh (1930-55), was equally progressive and active in spite of being partly paralysed. It was during his reign, in 1949, that Udaipur was absorbed into the newly formed state of Rajasthan. The present descendant of the Sisodia line is Sharji Arvind Singh Mewar.

FOLLOWING PAGES A panoramic sunset view of Udaipur, with Jag Niwas in the middle of Lake Pichola, and City Palace rising over the houses to the left.

BELOW The *tripolia*, or triple-arched gateway, leading to the outermost courtyard of City Palace is overlooked by Amar Vilas.

CITY PALACE

The principal residence of the Sisodias since its foundation in 1559 by Rana Udai Singh, the imposing City Palace in Udaipur is dramatically sited on the east side of the artifcial Lake Pichola. The complex comprises a sequence of gateways, audience halls, residential apartments and walled courts at successive levels. They are linked by narrow staircases and topped by rooftop terraces and pavilions, many of them looking out over the lake. These various parts of the royal complex were added during the 17th and 18th centuries by successive rulers to the core residence of Rana Udai Singh that is located at the southern extremity of the complex. The royal precinct begins with the *tripolia*, the triple-arched ceremonial gateway that leads to an open parade ground for troops and animals. To one side of the gateway is the multi-storey palace block, crowned by Amar Vilas, a garden court with apartments raised on massive walls that conceal a natural hill.

ABOVE The square, marble bathing pool in
Badi Mahal is surrounded by arcades; beyond
lies the garden courtyard of Amar Vilas.

LEFT This painted photographic cut-out of Maharana Bhupal Singh is placed within an arched alcove in Pritam Niwas, a small reception hall in Udaipur's City Palace.

RIGHT A glass mosaic design in Badi Chatur Chowk, a private court at an upper level of City Palace dating from the early 18th century, shows a maiden carrying a tray of refreshments beside a flowering tree.

FAR RIGHT, ABOVE The walls of Badi Chatur Chowk are covered with coloured glass mosaic designs.

FAR RIGHT, BELOW Coloured European tiles clad the balconied sitting area that opens off Badi Chatur Chowk.

RIGHT The central chamber of Kanch ki Burj is walled with chevron patterns in coloured glass; mirrors cloak the floor as well as the fluted dome above.

SHIV NIWAS

Work on Shiv Niwas was begun by Maharana Sajjan Shambhu Singh (1874-84), and completed by his successor, Maharana Fateh Singh, at the beginning of the 20th century. Standing to the immediate south of Udaipur's City Palace, Shiv Niwas was intended as a royal guest house. Its three levels of apartments are arranged in a grand semicircular arc around an internal court, in the middle of which is a marble pool sheltered by a tree. Balconies and rooftop terraces opening off different bedroom suites enjoy serene views: to the south are the gardens laid out below the dam wall of Lake Pichola; to the west, the island resorts of Jag Mandir and Jag Niwas. The principal reception room at courtyard level has a projecting window alcove that also benefts from a lakeside view. The palace now functions as a deluxe hotel run by the present representative of the Sisodia family, Sharji Arvind Singh Mewar, whose own residence backs onto the hotel.

RIGHT A rooftop terrace in Shiv Niwas, with a distant view of Jag Niwas and the hills surrounding Lake Pichola.

LEFT An internal balcony with inlaid coloured glass decoration in the principal reception room of Shiv Niwas, Udaipur.

ABOVE Low chairs and tables crafted from Belgian crystal furnish the principal reception room; a portrait of Maharana Sajjan Shambhu Singh is seen on the wall behind.

ABOVE LEFT Two exquisite details from the inlaid coloured glass panel that runs around the lower walls of the reception room, depicting tigers, lions, and hunting dogs in a fanciful forested setting.

JAG MANDIR

Scenically located on an island in the middle of Lake Pichola in Udaipur, Jag Mandir was built in 1620 by Rana Karan Singh as a pleasure resort for his family members and courtiers. It provided refuge to Prince Khurram (the future emperor Shah Jahan), who lived here for a few months in 1627-28 after his rebellion against his father Jahangir was thwarted. It is sometimes believed that this future builder of the Taj Mahal at Agra may have been influenced by Gul Mahal, the white marble pavilion on Jag Mandir where he supposedly stayed. The triple-storey Gul Mahal, together with three other lesser pavilions and lines of open arcades with sculpted elephants, faces a formal garden. Its waterways and fountains were added by Rana Jagat Singh I in the middle of the 17th century. Jag Mandir continued to be used as a pleasure resort by the later Sisodias, and it served as a place of shelter for British families during the uprising of 1857. Visitors arriving by boat continue to enjoy the luminescent beauty of the island.

LEFT The arcades, terraces and domed pavilions of this picturesque island resort seem afloat over Lake Pichola.

RIGHT The domed chamber in the uppermost level of Gul Mahal is entirely cloaked in white marble inlaid with delicate polychrome designs.

BELOW The lily pond in one of the outer courtyards of Jag Niwas is edged with fanciful petal-like designs carved out of stone.

JAG NIWAS

Known the world over as Lake Palace Hotel, Jag Niwas in Udaipur was laid out by Rana Jagat Singh II in 1746 as the second island resort on Lake Pichola, after Jag Mandir. The garden palace proved an ideal setting for boating parties, picnics, musical performances and other courtly entertainments. After falling into disrepair for many years, it was saved from further deterioration by Bhagwat Singh (1955-84), who restored and enlarged the original pavilions of the palace in order to create a five-star luxury hotel. The renovated palace opened in 1963, immediately attracting an international clientele that included many world celebrities. Benefiting from an incomparable setting and an imaginative and immaculately recreated Rajput atmosphere, Jag Niwas still preserves the traditional pattern of interior courtyards surrounded by formal reception rooms and private apartments. Many of these have balconies that take advantage of the breathtaking views of City Palace on the main shore.

ABOVE This recently restored bedroom has a swing hanging from the ceiling painted with a monsoon sky. A portrait of Maharana Swarup Singh (1842-61) adorns the wall.

AMET HAVELI

This modest but charming waterside mansion in Udaipur is located on a promontory opposite Jag Niwas. It takes its name from the Amet family, which traces its ancestry back to the Sisodia line itself, and was prominent at the Udaipur court in the 18th and 19th centuries. Serving for a time as the city residence of the Amet *thakurs*, the *haveli* gradually fell into disuse over the years as the family declined in importance. In the early 1990s, it was restored by a Spanish decorator, who had the building repaired and whitewashed. The restrained colour scheme and the choice of furnishings, many of them eclectic and non-Indian in origin, create a spare and calming ambience that complements the reflecting waters of the surrounding lake. The reception room of the *haveli* opens off a walled garden with a central fountain that also contributes to the soothing atmosphere. This delightful mansion remains in private hands.

LEFT A balcony capped by a squat dome protrudes into Lake Pichola so as to catch the afternoon breeze.

RIGHT The austerity of the reception room, with its bare walls and white drapes, is relieved by a white cockatoo on a swing.

SAJJANGARH & SHIKARBADI

Sajjangarh is one of the many resorts of the Sisodias that dot the picturesque hills around Lake Pichola in Udaipur. Named after its founder, Maharana Sajjan Shambhu Singh (1874-84), the palace crowns one of the highest peaks in the vicinity, from where the king and his courtiers took pleasure in the striking views of the landscape and approaching monsoon storms. Though little is preserved of Sajjangarh's halls and apartments, the terraces still offer wonderful panoramas of the surrounding landscape.

The Sisodias and their nobles indulged their love of hunting by shooting tiger, leopard and boar in the wooded ranges outside Udaipur. One of the lodges built for this purpose is Shikarbadi, a royal hunting villa 5 kilometres south of the city. It dates from the 1940s, during the reign of Maharana Bhupal Singh, and still retains its original, European-inspired furnishings. The villa now functions as a small hotel.

LEFT A bird's-eye view of Udaipur and Lake Pichola from the upper terrace of Sajjangarh.

RIGHT The staircase foyer in Shikarbadi is dominated by a Belgian crystal chandelier; a silver warrior on horseback graces a small table in the centre of the room.

KUMBHALGARH

The impregnable fortress of Kumbhalgarh is located above a strategic pass in the forested ranges of Aravalli Hills, 90 kilometres north of Udaipur. Named after Rana Kumbha of Chittaurgarh who built its colossal walls in the 15th century, Kumbhalgarh was the most important defensive outpost on the northern frontier of the Mewar (Udaipur) kingdom. It was here that the infant Udai Singh, who later established the city of Udaipur, was brought to safety after an attempt on his life in 1536. While several temples and memorial *chhatris* stand inside the walls of Kumbhalgarh, no palace survives from the period of either Rana Kumbha or Udai Singh. Badal Mahal, a small palace crowning the summit of this mountain stronghold, more than 1,000 metres above sea level, is associated with Maharana Fateh Singh, dating no earlier than the beginning of the 20th century. This modest structure, now somewhat dilapidated but with traces of its original painted decoration, is mainly of interest for its spectacular setting.

LEFT The broad ramparts of Kumbhalgarh served as a walkway for soldiers. Stepping up the side of the hill, they lead up to Badal Mahal at the summit of the fortress.

BELOW LEFT Windows in a domed corner tower of Badal Mahal offer commanding views of the landscape.

BELOW & BOTTOM The interior apartments of Badal Mahal still preserve original colours.

BELOW LEFT The newly refurbished *jali* screen has geometric patterns filled with brightly coloured glass.

BELOW A mural at the entrance to the Gokulajara apartment depicts three Rajput maidens under a willow.

BELOW RIGHT The Ranjit Prakash Suite has a game of *parchesi* laid out on a mirrored table, and a cushioned sitting area at the far end.

DEOGARH MAHAL

Dating back to 1670, this palace is situated within a hilltop fort in the middle of Deogarh town, 135 kilometres north of Udaipur. Deogarh in the Aravalli Hills was the headquarters of a small estate granted to Rawat Dwarka Das in 1692 by the Sisodia ruler Rana Jai Singh II. Dwarka Das was a Chundawat *thakur* who traced his ancestry to the 15th-century Sisodia ruler Chundaji. He founded Deogarh Mahal, which was much expanded in later times by his descendants, who were responsible for the many fne murals that adorn the interior apartments. These paintings testify to a local but signifcant school of art that fburished here in the 18th and 19th centuries. The palace is reached after passing through a gateway positioned between the bastions in the fort walls. The gateway leads to a court, on one side of which stands the main three-storey wing of the palace, with private apartments arranged around an upper terrace. The palace has now been converted into a hotel.

RIGHT The ceiling of the sitting room in the Gokulajara apartment is covered with inlaid work of coloured glass, creating intricate geometric and foliate patterns.

FOLLOWING PAGES Colourful glass panels entirely cloak the surfaces of the *shish mahal*. The raised sitting areas on two sides are reserved for conversation and smoking.

BELOW Multi-storey apartments in Rana Kumbha's Palace, topped by *chhatris*, are arrayed around a sequence of inner courts, all contained within the fortified perimeter wall.

LEFT Steps ascend to an apartment roofed with a pointed vault in Rana Kumbha's Palace; the balconies that once projected from the windows have mostly fallen.

BELOW Ruins of a multi-storey residence outside the walls of Rana Kumbha's Palace.

CHITTAURGARH

The capital of Mewar until the move to Udaipur (115 kilometres west) in 1559, Chittaurgarh traces its turbulent history back to the 8th century when it served as the headquarters of the Guhilot warriors, remote ancestors of the Sisodias. Chittaurgarh is noted in Rajput history for the disastrous assaults of 1303, 1535 and 1568, the last by Akbar who headed the Mughal forces. Its massive ramparts and defensive gateways that ring the long, flat-topped hill are attributed to Rana Kumbha, the famous mid-15th century Sisodia ruler, as is the largest palace within its walls. The oldest example of royal architecture in Rajasthan, Rana Kumbha's Palace is entered on the east through a *tripolia* gateway. This leads to a large outer court overlooked by a columned audience hall on one side. Though largely abandoned after 1568, Chittaurgarh was on occasions occupied by the Udaipur maharanas who built several small palaces here in the 19th and early 20th centuries.

LEFT This comparatively well-preserved apartment in Rana Kumbha's Palace served as the residence of his son and heir.

FOLLOWING PAGES The diminutive Padmini Palace in the middle of a tank at Chittaurgarh was built at the turn of the 20th century by Maharana Fateh Singh. It is named after the Sisodia queen whose beauty is said to have so captivated Alauddin Khalji, sultan of Delhi, that he launched the violent siege of 1303.

149

BELOW The inner court of Karni Fort with its upper level apartments and arcaded balconies.

BELOW RIGHT Interior colonnades of Castle Bijaipur, with paired columns and lobed arches in the Mughal style.

KARNI FORT, BAMBORA & CASTLE BIJAIPUR

Karni Fort in Bambora, 43 kilometres south-east of Udaipur, was the site of a crucial battle between Rana Sangram Singh of Udaipur and the Mughal army in 1711, in which the Sisodia ranas were triumphant. It was also the residence of the Sodawa *thakurs*, a family of nobles that served under the Sisodias in the 18th and 19th centuries. After the battle, a palace was erected within the fort. Although it has been converted into a hotel, the ramparts and lookout towers of the fort remain intact.

The same is true of Castle Bijaipur, a restored palace that is located about 120 kilometres east of Udaipur. Home of the descendants of Rao Vijay Singh, a celebrated 16th-century Sisodia warrior, the palace stands on top of a plateau, with striking panoramas of the surrounding landscape. The nearby forested wildlife sanctuary, once a royal hunting preserve of the Sisodias, has become popular with wildlife conservationist groups.

ABOVE The traditional sun emblem of the Sisodias of Udaipur painted on the façade of Castle Bijaipur.

ABOVE RIGHT An enclosed balcony supported by corbelled brackets on the façade of Castle Bijaipur.

BHAINSRORGARH

Though more than 200 kilometres east of Udaipur, the estate of Bhainsrorgarh formed part of the territories of the Sisodia maharanas, with whom the Bhainsrorgarh *thakurs* maintained close relations. In 1742, the estate was granted by Maharana Jagat Singh II to Rawat Lal Singh, who set about fortifying this site on a 70-metre high rocky ridge, overlooking the Chambal River. The work was partly financed by Jagat Singh who apparently allotted three days of income of the Udaipur kingdom towards its construction. Rawat Lal Singh was also responsible for erecting the various structures of the palace complex that occupies the fort, including Mardana Mahal for the rulers and his male retinues, and Zenana Mahal for the courtly women and children. There was even a separate granary structure. A later figure of the Bhainsrorgarh family is Rawat Inder Singh (1897-1946), who gained renown as an enthusiastic collector of horses.

LEFT The various buildings of the palace complex strung out along the rocky ridge above the Chambal River.

BELOW The whitewashed façade of Mardana Mahal, the principal wing of Bhainsrorgarh, has multiple projecting balconies on two levels overlooking the river.

BELOW RIGHT The arcaded living-dining room in Mardana Mahal has a curious life-size, cut-out figure of Rawat Inder Singh placed in a corner.

RIGHT A puja room in Mardana Mahal enshrines the figurines of Radha and Krishna, as well as that of Bayan Mataji, the protective goddess of the Bhainsrorgarh *thakurs*.

JUNA MAHAL, DUNGARPUR

In the hilly country in the extreme south of Rajasthan, 130 kilometres from Udaipur, is Dungarpur, capital of a small kingdom whose rulers claimed ancestral links with the Sisodias of Udaipur. Dungarpur was conquered in 1573 by the Mughal army, but nevertheless managed to retain some measure of independence. Maharawal Shiv Singh (1730-85), the most powerful Dungarpur ruler in later times, fought many battles against the invading Marathas. He was responsible for repairing the fort walls and extending the palace of Juna Mahal that nestles against a wooded hillside at the edge of the town. Like City Palace in Udaipur, its outer enclosure is entered through a *tripolia* gateway. The complex is dominated by the seven-storey Fateh Prakash dating back to the 17th century, which served as the *zenana*. This overlooks the formal reception rooms, including Darbar Hall and Am Khas, both of which were added by Shiv Singh. Colourful paintings adorn the interiors.

LEFT Murals in the Darbar Hall depict the Dungarpur rulers on hunting expeditions.

RIGHT Portraits of Maharanas Sajjan Shambhu Singh and Fateh Singh of Udaipur, with whom the Dungarpur maharawals maintained close connections, are displayed on a wall in the Darbar Hall.

FOLLOWING PAGES The brightly painted columns, walls and ceiling of the Darbar Hall create a vibrant setting.

BELOW English plates with a popular
Chinese blue-and-white pattern decorate
an alcove in Am Khas, a reception room
in Dungarpur's Juna Mahal.

LEFT The ceiling of this apartment in Juna
Mahal has a central mirrored panel with
rings that once held a swing. The panel is
surrounded by painted scenes of Krishna
dancing with the *gopis*.

BELOW The four-storey Ek Thambia Mahal
stands in an empty pool in the middle of
the central courtyard of Udai Bilas.

UDAI BILAS, DUNGARPUR

Picturesquely situated at the edge of
a lake, only a short distance from the
town of Dungarpur, is Udai Bilas, the
new residence of the Dungarpur rulers
after they moved from Juna Mahal.
The palace is named after its founder,
Maharawal Udai Singh II (1845-98). The
principal wing of the palace has a central
square courtyard around which formal
reception and banquet rooms are
arranged. Ek Thambia Mahal, a curious
four-storey pleasure pavilion, stands
freely in the middle of the courtyard.
Unique in the palace architecture of
Rajasthan, the tower comprises two
superimposed chambers raised on a
colonnade, and topped by a *chhatri*, all
connected by a spiral staircase. Its outer
walls are exquisitely carved in different
coloured stones. Udai Bilas was
substantially refurbished by Maharawal
Lakshman Singh (1918-89), and now
functions as a hotel. The original
residential block at the rear of the
courtyard, however, is still occupied by
the Dungarpur royal family.

RIGHT In Ek Thambia Mahal, a curving
bangla cornice overhangs an immaculately
carved stone window with wooden shutters
and dancing maiden brackets in white marble.

FOLLOWING PAGES, LEFT A room with
a mirrored floor in Udai Bilas stands shorn
of its original furnishings.

FOLLOWING PAGES, RIGHT The spiral
staircase at the ground level of Ek Thambia
Mahal gives access to the chambers above.

BUNDI & KOTA

Tucked away in the wooded hills of south-eastern Rajasthan, the kingdom of Bundi was governed by Hada Rajputs. These rulers trace their origins to Hada Raj, a warrior of the Chauhan clan who was killed in 1022 fighting Mahmud of Ghazni, when this Afghan conqueror passed through Rajasthan on his way to pillage the great Hindu temple at Somnath in Gujarat. Rao Deva, a descendant of Hada Raj, wrested Bundi from the local Mina chiefs in 1342, thereby initiating a line of rulers that has endured to this day. Over the next two hundred years or so, the Bundi chiefs came under the influence of their more powerful neighbours, the Sisodias of Chittaurgarh. They assisted the Sisodias in times of war, and intermarried with them. The accession of Rao Surjan (1554-85) ushered in a new era in the history of Bundi; he surrendered to Akbar the fort at Ranthambhor, which he had governed on behalf of the Sisodias, and was rewarded with territories that substantially augmented the Bundi kingdom. Thereafter, Surjan and his successors served with considerable success under the Mughals.

During the reign of Rao Rattan Singh (1607-31), the trusted commander of Jahangir, the Bundi kingdom was partitioned by the creation of the independent state of Kota. Even so, Rattan Singh retained sufficient territories and funds to initiate construction work on the Garh Palace above Bundi. Rao Chhattar Sal (1631-58), the next ruler, participated in the Mughal battles in the Deccan in peninsular India, as did his son, Rao Bhao Singh (1658-78), who governed Aurangabad on behalf of Aurangzeb. A bitter feud with Jaipur broke out under the reign of his successor, Rao Budh Singh, who was expelled from his kingdom by the Kachhawaha forces. It was not until the rule of Umed Singh I (1748-70) that the raos once again occupied Bundi. Difficulties persisted with Jaipur, and relations with Udaipur soured, especially after Rao Ajit Singh accidentally killed Rana Ari Singh of Udaipur on a hunting expedition in 1773.

Under Rao Bishan Singh (1773-1821), the Bundi dominions were ravaged by the Maratha troops, and the ruler was compelled to pay tribute. By 1817, Bishan Singh was only too willing to sign a treaty with the British East India Company that guaranteed protection from the invaders. Raja Ram Singh (1821-89), the next maharao, was well respected by the British and fellow Rajputs. A conservative and religious person, he established Sanskrit schools, and also initiated economic and administrative reforms. He was succeeded by Maharao Raghubir Singh (1889-1927), his adopted son, who enthusiastically supported the British during World War I. A later ruler, Bahadur Singh, was a distinguished military figure. Before his accession to the Bundi throne in 1945, he had earned the Military Cross from the British for his gallantry during the Burma campaign in World War II. Ranjit Singh is the present representative of the Bundi family.

Situated only 38 kilometres south-east of Bundi, Kota was the capital of an independent state of the same name, its first ruler being Rao Madho Singh, son of Rao Rattan Singh of Bundi. The kingdom of Kota was carved out of Bundi in 1624, when Jahangir made over its territories to Madho Singh. This ruler had assisted the Mughal army at a time when Jahangir's son, Prince Khurram, was threatening rebellion. Thereafter, Bundi and Kota developed in parallel though not always harmonious directions. Madho Singh, whose rule extended up to 1648, was succeeded by a series of rulers who served under the Mughals, most of them perishing in battle in the Deccan. One of these rulers, Bhim Singh I (1707-20), was the first of the Kota kings to bear the title of 'maharao'. He successfully extended the Kota dominions without antagonizing his more powerful neighbour, Maharaja Sawai Jai Singh II of Jaipur. However, incursions by the Jaipur forces into Kota's domains occurred during the reigns of Maharaos Durjan Sal (1724-56) and Chhattar Sal I (1759-66). Towards the end of the 18th century, the Marathas invaded the southern portions of Kota, and the maharaos had to pay a hefty tribute in order to induce them to withdraw.

The reign of the next significant Kota ruler, Maharao Umed Singh I (1771-1819), who assumed the throne as an infant, was dominated by Zalim Singh, his powerful and capable regent. He guided Kota back to prosperity by introducing a stable form of government, a new system of taxation, and a European training method for the army. As the effective representative of the state, Zalim Singh signed an agreement in 1818 with the East India Company, thus safeguarding Kota's territories from Maratha invasion. The following years were marred by rivalries between the Kota maharaos and the descendants of Zalim Singh. The situation was only resolved in 1838, during the reign of Maharao Ram Singh II (1827-66), when the British insisted that the separate state of Jhalawar be created to the south of Kota for Zalim Singh's family. Financial difficulties in Kota intensified under Maharao Chhattar Sal II (1866-89), until a prime minister was appointed by the British to pay off state debts and overhaul the administration. Chhattar Sal's adopted son and successor, Maharao Umed Singh II (1889-1940), was responsible for improving the fortunes of the kingdom and relations with the British. At India's independence, Maharao Bhim Singh II was on the Kota throne, and he did much to develop Kota into an industrial and commercial centre. The present representative of the Kota royal family is Brijraj Singh.

PRECEDING PAGES A view of Bundi Garh Palace, with its commanding ramparts rising steeply up the hill above the city.

BELOW LEFT This painting in Chitra Shala shows an amorous prince in a private garden within the palace.

BELOW Murals depicting courtly scenes cover the walls of Chitra Shala.

BUNDI GARH PALACE

This palace has been the residence of the Bundi rulers since the early 17th century, when Rattan Singh and Chhattar Sal first began work on its ramparts. Among the features dating from this time are Hathi Pol, a gateway with elephant sculptures through which the complex is entered, and the first inner court overlooked by a columned audience hall and white marble throne. Several of the quarters for the ruler and his family, such as Chitra Shala and Badal Mahal, belong to the same period, but were renovated towards the end of the 18th century during the reign of Rao Umed Singh I. The same is true of Chhattar Mahal, a private reception hall at the upper level that takes its name from Rao Chhattar Sal. All the apartments in the palace are adorned with paintings portraying the Bundi rulers and their retinues, as well as diverse subjects from Hindu mythology. These murals testify to a vigorous school of painting that fburished in Bundi in the 18th and 19th centuries.

RIGHT Arcades lining the courtyard of Chitra Shala are adorned with figural and decorative paintings.

LEFT BELOW In this mural in Chhattar Mahal at Bundi Garh Palace, the men of the Bundi cavalry are seen wearing a variety of turbans and riding horses of different colours.

BELOW A Chitra Shala mural shows Rao Umed Singh I mounted on a warhorse, leading his foot soldiers into battle.

RIGHT The innermost reception room of Badal Mahal has its walls and faceted vault covered with paintings. Many depict mythological scenes, such as Krishna and Radha seated in a horse-drawn chariot.

SUKH NIWAS &
PHUL SAGAR PALACE

The wooded hills surrounding Bundi are dotted with artifcial lakes, some with small pleasure resorts. Rao Bishan Singh built the palace of Sukh Niwas on the dam wall of Jait Sagar, a lake he created in the hills just north of the city in the 1770s. He and his successors used Sukh Niwas as a picnic spot as well as a base for hunting expeditions in the nearby forests. Its most famous visitor was Rudyard Kipling, who noted his stay here in his travel diaries.

Phul Sagar, a lake 10 kilometres north-west of Bundi, dates from the period of Rao Bhao Singh in the second half of the 17th century, as does the palace that he built here for one of his favourite concubines. Little remains of the original building, which was entirely refurbished in 1945 in the latest European manner, complete with exuberant Modernist furniture and murals. It is still used by the current representative of the Bundi royal family as a restful lakeside retreat.

BELOW Eccentric Modernist murals executed by Italian artists interned in India during World War II adorn the dining room of Phul Sagar Palace.

LEFT The domed pavilions of the rooftop terrace in Sukh Niwas overlook the waters of Jait Sagar, a short distance outside Bundi.

BELOW Naya Darwaza serves as the principal entrance to Kota Fort Palace.

KOTA FORT PALACE

Standing in a walled citadel that lines the bank of the Chambal River running through the middle of Kota, the fort palace dates back to the foundation of the city by Rao Madho Singh in 1624. The earliest parts of the complex are the lofty red sandstone ramparts and Hathi Pol, the gateway leading to the main block. This contains Raj Mahal, the principal reception hall where the Kota rulers held darbar. Private apartments overlooking the river, such as Bada Mahal, also date back to the 17th century. The complex was expanded and substantially refurbished by Maharaos Bhim Singh I and Durjan Sal in the early decades of the 18th century. Under Maharao Ram Singh II, in the mid-19th century, Raj Mahal and Bada Mahal were adorned with murals portraying the Kota rulers and their retinues in the palace, undertaking pleasurable excursions to the gardens outside the city, or going on boat rides on the Chambal. These rival the Bundi paintings in range and liveliness.

RIGHT This cushioned seat beneath a canopy supported by slender silver pillars in Raj Mahal was meant exclusively for the Kota ruler. The walls around are crowded with murals illustrating courtly themes.

BELOW LEFT Chairs are lined up beneath lobed arcades in Bhim Mahal, the private audience chamber in Kota Fort Palace.

BELOW Flying celestials embellish the ceiling of Arjun Mahal, an 18th-century hall in the fort palace.

ABOVE Miniature paintings on paper, framed in glass, are set into the walls of Bada Mahal, another apartment in the fort palace.

RIGHT This polygonal alcove in Bhim Mahal now serves as a bedchamber.

UMED BHAWAN

Umed Bhawan on the outskirts of Kota was the preferred private residence of Maharao Umed Singh II, who moved here in 1905 from the more central fort palace. Named after this royal patron who commissioned it, the palace is a fne example of the revived Rajput style promoted by Samuel Swinton Jacob, the British engineer based in Jaipur. Its somewhat severe exterior is relieved by verandas and porches with arcades of pointed, lobed arches, and corner octagonal towers topped by diminutive *chhatris*, all of which are typical of Jacob's designs. Umed Bhawan's interior is arranged around a pair of courtyards, the larger one leading to formal reception rooms, including the double-height Darbar Hall with lobed arcades. The revived Rajput manner of this hall contrasts with the European style of the Blue Lounge and Billiard Room, the latter with hunting trophies fxed to the walls. A part of the palace has now been converted into a hotel.

LEFT The arcaded veranda at the upper level displays fine stone carving, particularly in the perforated designs above the lobed arches.

RIGHT The Blue Lounge, now a hotel lobby, is divided into two by a great curving arch; the furniture, drapes, lamps and chandelier were all imported from Europe.

JODHPUR

The desert expanse of Marwar in western Rajasthan was ruled by the Rathors, whose capital Jodhpur was founded in 1459 by Rao Jodha (1438-88), a Rajput warrior. From the fort that he built (later known as Mehrangarh) on a vast, rocky outcrop rising dramatically above the city, Jodha and his descendants ruled over what was the largest of all Rajput kingdoms. In 1542, Rao Maldev, ruler of Jodhpur from 1532 to 1562, gave safe passage to the Mughal ruler Humayun on his flight from Sher Shah, the Afghan warrior who had usurped the Delhi throne. In retaliation, Sher Shah raided Jodhpur in 1544. Twenty years later, the kingdom was invaded once again, this time by Akbar, who was intent on establishing Mughal supremacy in north India. Jodhpur remained under nominal Mughal control until Raja Udai Singh (1581-95) formally acknowledged Akbar's sovereignty in 1583. After offering his daughter in marriage to Akbar's son, Prince Salim (the future emperor Jahangir), Udai Singh became one of Akbar's favourite commanders, and was permitted to use the title of 'raja'. This newly forged relationship with the Mughals led to a welcome period of stability and prosperity for Jodhpur.

Udai Singh's son, Sawai Raja Sur Singh (1595-1619), was an esteemed figure at the courts of Akbar and Jahangir, accompanying the Mughal forces on their campaigns in Gujarat and the Deccan. His successor, Maharaja Gaj Singh I (1619-38), also served under Shah Jahan, and was even present at the emperor's coronation ceremony in Agra. The next ruler, Maharaja Jaswant Singh I (1638-78), was for a time the governor of Malwa, leading Shah Jahan's forces against his rebellious son, the future Aurangzeb. Once Aurangzeb seized the Mughal throne, Jaswant Singh's power was severely curtailed and he was sent as governor to the Afghan border. Jaswant Singh's death in 1678 was followed by an era of rebellion and intrigue at the Jodhpur court, leading to a second occupation of Marwar by the Mughal forces. It was only after Aurangzeb's death in 1707, almost thirty years later, that Maharaja Ajit Singh (1707-24) was finally able to capture Jodhpur. Relations between the Rathors and the Mughals improved after Ajit Singh's daughter married the emperor, Farrukh Siyar. Soon after, another of his daughters married the Kachhawaha ruler, Maharaja Sawai Jai Singh II, thereby securing an alliance with Jaipur.

Events took a turn for the worse when Ajit Singh was murdered by his son Bakhta Singh, although it was Bakhta's brother, Abhai Singh (1725-49), who actually assumed the Jodhpur throne. The following years witnessed harassment by the Marathas who raided Marwar in 1736, retreating only after being paid off with large sums of money.

The next ruler of note, Maharaja Bijaya Singh (1752-92), spent much of his long reign defending Marwar from the Marathas, and subduing his rebellious nobles. The situation was brought under control only during the period of Maharaja Man Singh (1803-43), though the early years of his long reign were marred by quarrels with Udaipur over a marital alliance, and also with Jaipur after the massacre of several followers of the Kachhawaha ruler at Nagaur in the Jodhpur kingdom. By this time, however, the East India Company was an established presence in north India, and in 1839 an army commanded by Colonel Sutherland entered Marwar. Thereafter, Jodhpur was forced to accept the presence of a British Resident who influenced affairs of the kingdom. The reigns of the next maharaja, the adopted Takhat Singh (1843-73), and his successors were marked by unprecedented peace and prosperity, partly due to the introduction of judicial, educational and social reforms. While the Jodhpur throne passed to Takhat Singh's eldest son, and in turn to his descendants, it was Takhat Singh's third son, Pratap Singh, who emerged as the dominant personality of the era. Born in 1845, he served as regent under the next three rulers. Pratap Singh was famous for his sporting and hunting skills, and his ability to command the Jodhpur Lancers, the valiant military contingent that served under the British in China during the Boxer uprising, and in Europe, Egypt and the Middle East during World War I. Sir Pratap Singh, as he came to be titled, welcomed three Princes of Wales to Jodhpur, and attended Queen Victoria's Golden and Diamond Jubilees as well as Edward VII's coronation in London. He even gained renown by bringing the first Indian polo team to England.

By the time of Pratap Singh's death in 1922, Maharaja Umaid Singh (1918-47) was ruling over a progressive kingdom with an efficient administration. An enthusiastic polo player, he also loved flying, and it was thanks to him that Jodhpur served as an important military base in World War II. Umaid Singh's famine relief policy gave rise to the immense Umaid Bhawan and a dam that remains Jodhpur's principal source of water; both projects employed thousands of workers. In 1949, during the reign of Maharaja Hanwant Singh (1947-52), Jodhpur was absorbed into the new state of Rajasthan. Hanwant Singh died tragically young in an air accident, and was succeeded by Gaj Singh II, known affectionately as Bapji, who was only four years old when he became representative of the Rathor royal line. In his early career, Gaj Singh served as a diplomat and parliamentarian; today he is fully committed to his various charitable trusts in education, medicine and heritage.

PRECEDING PAGES The formidable ramparts of Mehrangarh are dramatically perched on top of a long sandstone bluff.

BELOW The screened balconies of Zenana Chowk were intended for women to discreetly observe the activities below.

MEHRANGARH

Headquarters of the Rathor Rajputs since the foundation of Jodhpur in the mid-15th century, Mehrangarh is dominated by a circuit of massive ramparts, with the blue city of Jodhpur spread out below. The palace within is approached from the north, along a ramp that passes through a sequence of strongly defended, arched gateways. Most of the palace is assigned to the reigns of Maharajas Jaswant Singh I and Ajit Singh, which preceded and followed respectively the Mughal occupation of the fort from 1678 to 1707. There were, however, substantial additions in later times, especially in the 19th century. The principal reception halls are arranged around Daulat Khana and Singhar Chowks, a pair of courts separated by Janki Mahal, a residential wing. Corridors from here lead to Phul Mahal, the private audience hall of the palace. The other residential apartments beyond are disposed around Zenana Chowk. Stores, tanks and gardens occupy the remainder of the fortifed zone.

RIGHT Sati hand prints commemorating the ritual immolation of the widows of valiant Jodhpur princes are sculpted on the side walls of Loha Pol, or Iron Gate, leading to the palace in Mehrangarh.

ABOVE This alcove in Phul Mahal at Jodhpur's Mehrangarh palace, was sumptuously appointed by Maharaja Takhat Singh in the second half of the 19th century; his portrait appears in the half-dome above.

LEFT The ornamented royal bedchamber in Takhat Vilas, the private apartment of Takhat Singh, with the original *pankha* (fan) and mirrored glass globes above.

BELOW The imposing west front of Umaid
Bhawan is punctuated by towers, and topped
by a dome rising 56 metres above the central
rotunda; steps lead from the colonnaded
portico to the elegantly landscaped garden.

UMAID BHAWAN

This colossal palace on the southern
fringe of Jodhpur is named after its
founder, Maharaja Umaid Singh, who
in 1925 commissioned the London
architectural frm of Lanchester and
Lodge to design for him a new
residence in the fashionable Art Deco
style. Umaid Bhawan is monumentally
conceived on the grandest possible
scale, with residential wings fanning out
in a symmetrical fashion from a central
rotunda roofed by an imposing dome.
The rotunda is reached after passing
through an elliptical staircase hall,
with the ballroom and banquet hall on
either side. The palace is entirely built
in golden yellow sandstone, a material
that imbues its Modernist form with an
unmistakable Indian spirit. After ffteen
years of construction, the project was
fnally completed in 1943; however,
Umaid Singh lived here for only four
years. Although one half of Umaid
Bhawan is now a luxury hotel, the palace
continues to serve as the principal
residence of the Jodhpur royal family.

RIGHT The dome of the rotunda is capped
by a finial carved with a quartet of kites,
the sacred bird of the Rathor Rajputs.

FOLLOWING PAGES The elliptical entrance
hall of Umaid Bhawan has a double flight
of steps leading up to private apartments;
kites are sculpted onto columns at the
base of the banisters.

BELOW Coloured marble floor strips in the central rotunda of Jodhpur's Umaid Bhawan lead to sixteen finely worked sandstone piers overlooked by a gallery.

BELOW Coloured marble floor strips in the central rotunda of Jodhpur's Umaid Bhawan lead to sixteen finely worked sandstone piers overlooked by a gallery.

ABOVE The monumental ballroom is roofed with a neo-Classical, coffered barrel vault.

BELOW LEFT The corridor in the private wing of Jodhpur's Umaid Bhawan has a French crystal fountain, set in a shallow pool.

BOTTOM LEFT The Darbar Hall in the private wing has murals by the Polish artist, Julius Stefan Norblin, illustrating legendary heroes from Hindu mythology.

ABOVE The maharaja's bedroom in the private wing of the palace preserves its suite of Art Deco furniture and Norblin paintings.

ABOVE RIGHT The walls around the elegant swimming pool beneath the central wing of Umaid Bhawan are adorned with underwater motifs in cool blue tones.

ABOVE The maharaja's private sitting room in Jodhpur's Umaid Bhawan has paintings by Norblin and Art Deco chairs and couches upholstered in leopard skin.

RIGHT An engraved glass design by Norblin depicting the powerful goddess Kali dominates the gleaming pink-and-black bedroom of the maharani.

BELOW The inner courtyard is enclosed on all four sides by screened corridors leading to private apartments; an octagonal, domed chamber covers the roof at one end.

AJIT BHAWAN

This red sandstone palace on the outskirts of Jodhpur was built in 1929 by Maharaja Umaid Singh for his younger brother, Sir Ajit Singh, a prominent fgure at the Jodhpur court. When the British architect Henry Lanchester visited Jodhpur to supervise the construction of Umaid Bhawan, Ajit Singh consulted him on this project as well. The result was a revived Rajput style, quite unlike Umaid Bhawan's Art Deco manner. This traditional style was considered more appropriate for a palace intended as a private residence for a Jodhpur prince. Accordingly, it was furnished with fnely worked sandstone *jalis* and *chhatris*, especially around the courtyard at the core of the complex. When frst completed, Ajit Bhawan served as a hunting lodge for it was at the time surrounded by open country with plentiful game. Ajit Singh and his family eventually moved here permanently, and his descendants continue to occupy the premises. Part of the property now functions as a hotel.

ABOVE Enormous elephant tusks from Kenya flank the crystal bar that is conceived as a miniature domed pavilion.

ABOVE RIGHT Oil paintings of the Jodhpur rulers and an animal trophy adorn the principal sitting room.

BALSAMAND LAKE PALACE

Sitting atop the dam wall of Balsamand, an artifcial lake 8 kilometres north of Jodhpur, this palace with its waterside terraces and pavilions was intended for the Rathor maharajas and their family members, who often visited it in the monsoon season. Though frst established in the 17th century, the palace was much expanded in the late 19th century to accommodate the many women and children of the Rathor court who came here seeking relief from the desert heat of Jodhpur. Balsamand Lake Palace is built in a revived Rajput style, but on an intimate scale so as to achieve an unmistakable charm. Many of the apartments and reception rooms, together with their balconies, enjoy fne views of the lake, and their interiors are much enhanced by the light refecting from its waters. The Balsamand palace has been recently resuscitated so as to function as a small but refned hotel, thereby preserving something of its original purpose as a peaceful pleasure resort.

RIGHT The cool interiors of a bedroom in Balsamand Lake Palace.

NAGAUR FORT

Strategically sited on the Jodhpur-Delhi
road, Nagaur lies 135 kilometres north-
east of Jodhpur. The circular fort in
the middle of the town dates back to
the 12th century, when it was occupied
by the Chauhan Rajputs, ancestors
of several prominent royal families of
Rajasthan. After passing into the hands
of the Delhi sultans and then Akbar, who
used it as his principal headquarters in
Rajasthan, Nagaur Fort came into the
permanent possession of the Jodhpur
maharajas. In 1725, Maharaja Abhai
Singh presented the fort to his brother
Bakhta Singh, who had helped him gain
the Rathor throne by murdering their
father Ajit Singh. Bakhta Singh resided
in the fort until his death in 1752, laying
out an elaborate palace within the
ramparts, equipped with reception halls,
pleasure pavilions and a complex water
system. These buildings are arrayed
around a formal garden with terraces,
pools, water channels and fountains.
After falling into disrepair, these features
have now been fully restored.

LEFT Whitewashed pointed arches traverse
the double-height Abha Mahal, a private
reception hall at the core of the complex.

FOLLOWING PAGES The main terrace of
the palace in Nagaur Fort, with the multi-
storey Hadi Rani Mahal to the left, and
the columned audience hall to the right.

RIGHT Cloud-borne courtiers and maidens are painted on the ceiling of Akbari Mahal, one of the pavilions in the palace at Nagaur Fort.

BELOW The central chamber of the *hammam*, which opens off Abha Mahal, is roofed with a dome with an opening at its centre.

ABOVE Persian-styled winged angels are painted on the ceiling of an apartment in Hadi Rani Mahal.

BELOW The main sitting room, with its Art Deco fireplace, is dominated by family photographs and animal trophies.

SARDARSAMAND PALACE

Gazing out over Sardarsamand, an artifcial lake 55 kilometres south-east of Jodhpur, this palace was built in 1933 by Maharaja Umaid Singh, but named after his father Maharaja Sardar Singh. Umaid Singh intended it as a pleasure resort where visitors could relax among the trophies that he had brought back from his trips to Africa. The palace was designed in the fashionable Art Deco manner, but on a more intimate scale than Umaid Bhawan in Jodhpur. Even so, it is notable for its boldly styled, Modernist grey stone exterior with twin towers rising above the waters of the lake. The main building, housing the reception and dining rooms, was set in extensive grounds with facilities for swimming, tennis and squash; there was even a Japanese garden. Motorboat trips were also organized to see the flamingos on the lake during the winter season. Such royal diversions are available to guests of the hotel that has now been established within the palace grounds.

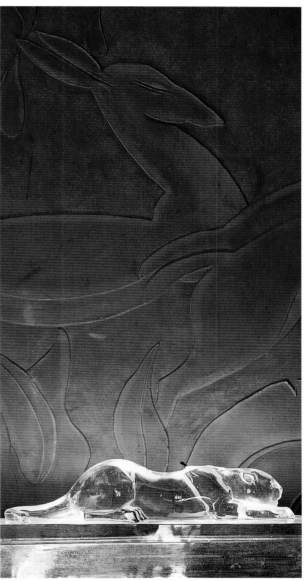

ABOVE LEFT Steel furniture in the bar is upholstered with panther skin, while a stuffed bear holds a circular table top.

ABOVE A glass sculpture of a reclining panther serves as a light in the dining room; the relief panel behind shows elegant, prancing deer.

ABOVE RIGHT The Art Deco bar with a stuffed deer head and a mural by Julius Stefan Norblin depicting an elephant locked in battle with a tiger.

FORT CHANWA, LUNI

Home of Kaviraj Muraridanji, a prominent noble at the Rathor court under Maharaja Jaswant Singh II in the last decades of the 19th century, Fort Chanwa is situated in the village of Luni, 36 kilometres south of Jodhpur. Muraridanji was a far-sighted administrator as well as an accomplished writer and poet, hence his title Kaviraj, or Poet Laureate. In 1894, he was rewarded for his services with the estate of Chanwa, on the sandy banks of Luni River, where he erected a fortified palace in a revived Rajput style. Like the residences of other *thakurs*, the building focused on an impressive, double-height Darbar Hall that opened off a central court and was surrounded by private apartments. Since Muraridanji lacked an heir, Fort Chanwa eventually passed into the control of the Jodhpur kingdom. Since 1948, it has been occupied by Dulip Singh, the youngest son of Umaid Singh, the maharaja of Jodhpur at the time. The palace has now been transformed into a tranquil hotel in a rural setting.

LEFT The Darbar Hall has a transverse arch supported on outsized lotus brackets; the triple-arcaded balcony at the rear is linked to a private gallery.

RIGHT The principal bedroom suite at the upper level has glass lamps and mirrored globes hanging from the ceiling.

BELOW LEFT Floor mattresses make for comfortable seating in the veranda that opens into a rooftop terrace.

BELOW An enamelled wash-basin and jug placed beneath a wall niche housing a sculpted Hindu divinity.

RAWLA NARLAI

The small town of Rawla Narlai lies nearly 160 kilometres south of Jodhpur, on the road to Udaipur. The palace here occupies the ruined fabric of a 16th-century fort in the middle of the town, behind which rises a great rocky hill. The palace itself, however, is not nearly so old, having been built by Swarup Singh, an influential *thakur* who maintained close relations with the Jodhpur rulers at the beginning of the 19th century. At its core is a walled garden courtyard overlooked by an arcaded veranda leading to a series of apartments. Some of the interiors were decorated with paintings, but these are badly faded. Since a game preserve of the Rathor maharajas was located only a short distance from Rawla Narlai, the palace here served as a hunting lodge for visiting royalty. It continued to fulfl this function under Maharaja Umaid Singh, who had it refurbished in the 1920s, though without restoring its paintings. It has now found a new lease of life as a small hotel.

RIGHT Wall and ceiling paintings in the bedroom of Maharaja Mahal portray trees, flowers and episodes from Krishna's life, with the youthful god playing the flute in the company of the *gopis*.

BIKANER

Occupying the sandy wasteland of north-west Rajasthan, Bikaner was the second largest Rajput kingdom after Jodhpur (Marwar), to which it owes its origin; indeed the two ruling houses were originally related. Bikaner is named after Bika (1465-1504), one of the sons of Rao Jodha of Jodhpur. With scant hope of inheriting the kingdom of his father, Bika left Jodhpur with several hundreds of his followers to capture a country of his own. In 1465, he settled on a desolate site that was to become the city of Bikaner, building a mud fort here that served as the headquarters of the future rulers. After Rao Jodha's death in 1488, Bika attempted to storm Mehrangarh in Jodhpur in the hope of seizing the Rathor throne, thus triggering a series of wars between the two states that waged for more than two hundred years.

Bika's descendants benefited from the weak rule of Suraj Mal, Jodha's successor at Jodhpur, and the general disruption caused by the invasion of north India in 1526 by the Mughal prince Babur. The Bikaner kingdom was consolidated and expanded under Jait Singh (1526-39), but he was slain by the forces of Rao Maldev of Jodhpur. Jait Singh's son, Kalyan Mal (1539-71), retired to Sirsa, about 250 kilometres away on the frontier of the Punjab, where he joined the forces of Sher Shah, the Afghan commander who expelled the Mughal ruler, Humayun, from India in 1540. As a member of Sher Shah's army, Kalyan Mal fought successfully against Rao Maldev in 1545, and subsequently recovered the territories lost by his father. The last years of Kalyan Mal's reign coincided with that of Akbar, to whom the Bikaner monarch formally submitted in 1570. Thus began the fruitful relationship between Bikaner and the Mughals.

Rai Singh (1571-1611), the next Bikaner monarch, rose to greatness in the service of Akbar and Jahangir, becoming one of the most influential of the Rajput nobles at the Mughal court. He was also an energetic builder, and he replaced Bika's mud fort in the middle of Bikaner with stone ramparts and gateways. Rai Singh's successors, Dalpat Singh (1611-31) and Karan Singh (1631-74), continued to serve the Mughal cause, the latter spending much of his career under Aurangzeb, subjugating the sultans of Bijapur and Golconda in the Deccan. It was, however, the next Bikaner king, Anup Singh (1674-98), who truly distinguished himself by leading the decisive assault on Golconda in 1687, for which feat Aurangzeb granted him the title of 'maharaja'. In spite of his prolonged absences from Bikaner, Anup Singh managed to promote a vibrant cultural life that proved to be the foundation of the city's efflorescence in the 18th century.

During the reign of Sujan Singh (1700-35) Bikaner broke off relations with the Mughals, and from 1719 onwards, this maharaja was based in the capital. Here, he successfully resisted an invasion by Abhai Singh of Jodhpur in 1733; even so, conflict with Jodhpur continued for the next twenty years. In 1739, Jodhpur attacked again, and Bikaner was only saved from occupation by the intervention of Maharaja Sawai Jai Singh II of Jaipur. Thereupon, Zorawar Singh, the maharaja of Bikaner from 1736 to 1746, forged an advantageous alliance with the Kachhawahas. The conflict with Jodhpur was finally resolved under Maharaja Gaj Singh (1746-87), but this was taken as a sign of weakness by the *thakurs* at the Bikaner court, and Gaj Singh had to devote some years suppressing their revolts. Despite this, his period is marked by considerable activity in the fields of art and architecture. The next maharaja, Surat Singh (1787-1828), attempted to maintain amiable relations with Jodhpur, but his reign was threatened by one last war with Marwar over a succession dispute, and further rebellions by his nobles. Surat Singh appealed to the East India Company for help, and in 1818 signed a treaty that fully restored his authority, though under the watchful eye of a British Resident. The following years witnessed the recovery of Bikaner's fortunes, and the forging of positive relations with the British, especially after the uprising of 1857 when the army of Maharaja Sardar Singh (1851-72), the next significant ruler, fought on the British side.

The reigns of Maharajas Dungar Singh (1872-87) and Ganga Singh (1887-1943) were marked by far-reaching reforms that transformed Bikaner into a model princely state. Ganga Singh spent two decades supervising the construction of a concrete canal that diverted water from the Sutlej River to Bikaner's desert lands. Other works included the building of railways, free hospitals and schools. Ganga Singh enjoyed the reputation of being one of the leading princes in India. He was popular with the British for his grouse shooting excursions, and played host to the Prince of Wales (the future George V), and a series of viceroys and governors. Ganga Singh led his celebrated Camel Corps to the Egyptian front and was one of the signatories of the Treaty of Versailles at the end of World War I. In 1921, he was the first Chancellor of the Chamber of Princes to be elected.

Ganga Singh was succeeded by Maharaja Sadul Singh (1943-47), who readily signed the accession of the princely states to the Union of India in 1947, but died before the merger of Bikaner with Rajasthan in 1949. His son and successor, Karni Singh (1947-88), was a historian as well as a celebrated marksman. The charitable trust that he established in the name of his grandfather is still active today. Narendra Singh is the current representative of the Bikaner royal family.

JUNAGARH

The imposing citadel of Junagarh in the middle of Bikaner has dominated the city since 1588 when Karan Chand, the capable minister of Rai Singh, undertook work on its stone ramparts. Completed in 1593, and originally named Chintamani, the high walls of the fort are protected by a broad moat. The palace within is entered from the east through Suraj Pol, beyond which lies a sequence of courtyards leading to Ganga Niwas and Vikram Vilas, the principal darbar halls of the complex. A smaller inner courtyard gives access to Anup Mahal, a lavishly decorated private audience chamber dating from the period of its royal builder, Anup Singh. Other halls and residential apartments such as Chandra and Chhatra Mahals are attributed to Maharajas Gaj Singh and Surat Singh in the late 18th and early 19th centuries. At the beginning of the 20th century, when the Bikaner rulers eventually shifted to Lallgarh Palace, Chintamani came to be known as Junagarh, or Old Fort.

PRECEDING PAGES Transverse arches support the wooden ceiling of Ganga Niwas, the majestic darbar hall at the core of Junagarh, added by Maharaja Ganga Singh in the early years of the 20th century.

LEFT The courtyard leading to Anup Mahal is paved in polychrome stonework; *jharokas* with screened windows conceal the upper rooms.

BELOW A World War I aeroplane, presented
to Maharaja Ganga Singh by the British,
is displayed in Vikram Vilas.

RIGHT A bedchamber in Chhatra Mahal, the uppermost apartment in Junagarh, has a tent-like wooden vault painted with scenes of Krishna dancing with the *gopis*.

FOLLOWING PAGES Chandra Mahal, the residential apartment intended for the royal family, is entirely decorated with coloured glass mosaic to create a gleaming interior.

LEFT Monsoon clouds are painted on the walls and ceiling of Badal Mahal, a ceremonial apartment in Bikaner's Junagarh dating from the late 19th century. A portrait of Maharaja Sardar Singh is painted on the side wall.

RIGHT Mughal-styled *jalis* illuminate the exquisitely painted foliate patterns in the Gaj Mandir corridor, leading to the *zenana* in Junagarh.

BELOW The private dining room in
Shiv Vilas, one of the residential wings
in Lallgarh, is almost overwhelmed by
the crowded display of hunting trophies.

LALLGARH

Built in 1901 for the young maharaja,
Ganga Singh, after his return from
Ajmer's Mayo College, Lallgarh in
Bikaner is the masterpiece of Samuel
Swinton Jacob. Encouraged to live
here by the British Resident who was
anxious to remove the impressionable
maharaja from the *zenana* intrigues of
the nearby Junagarh, Ganga Singh
became personally involved in the design
of Lallgarh, insisting on European-styled
interiors and lavish fittings. Despite that,
much of the exterior is in the revived
Rajput manner perfected by Jacob,
with exquisitely worked *jalis*, balconies
and balustrades, all fashioned out of
the deep red sandstone typical of
Bikaner. Completed in 1926, the
complex is laid out around a pair
of interior courtyards that provide
separate access to the public and
private zones within. Even though the
palace still functions as the principal
residence of the Bikaner royal family,
two wings have now been transformed
into independent hotels.

LEFT *Jali* windows and a rooftop pavilion
in the court leading to the Darbar Hall.

LEFT Swarna Mahal, a private reception room in Bikaner's Lallgarh, is decorated in a hybrid Rajput-European manner.

ABOVE Winged angels in blue monsoon clouds are painted on the underside of the arches in Swarna Mahal.

ABOVE RIGHT Even the electric switch on the wall in Swarna Mahal is integrated into the delicately worked decor.

233

BHANWAR NIWAS

In times past, Bikaner offered a safe
haven for merchants involved in the
caravan trade across the Rajasthan
desert. The wealthiest of these traders
erected lavish *havelis* that rival Junagarh
in the splendour of their decoration.
The largest and most elaborately
appointed *havelis* are those of the
Rampuria family, clustered together in
the narrow lanes of the old walled city
of Bikaner. They include Bhanwar Niwas,
built in 1927 by Seth Bhanwarlal, heir
to a lucrative textile and real estate
business in Calcutta. He is reputed to
have spent 350,000 rupees on its
construction, importing large quantities
of Italian marble for this purpose. Seth
Bhanwarlal had a weakness for European
furniture, paintings and cars, and the
architecture of Bhanwar Niwas is
obviously inspired by prevalent European
styles. After his death in 1947, his
descendants chose to live in Calcutta.
The family has recently decided to open
a major part of the *haveli* as a hotel.

LEFT Neo-Gothic arches and Italianate
balustrades, and floral swags enhance the
façade of the central courtyard.

RIGHT Portrait of Seth Bhanwarlal, displayed
prominently on the staircase landing.

BELOW Projecting windows and rooftop pavilions of Dungar Niwas's central block enjoy fine views of the lake.

DUNGAR NIWAS, GAJNER

The palace at Gajner, 32 kilometres south-west of Bikaner, was the setting for Maharaja Ganga Singh's famous grouse shooting parties, to which British dignitaries as well as Rajput royal fgures eagerly sought invitations. It is picturesquely set in lush gardens beside an artifcial lake that dates back to the 18th century, when Maharaja Gaj Singh used a small pavilion nearby as a hunting lodge and pleasure resort. The present building, however, was only begun in 1910 to designs by Samuel Swinton Jacob, Ganga Singh's favourite architect. It is a sprawling affair with residential wings fanning out from a central block that overlooks the lake. Like Jacob's Lallgarh, the palace has a profusion of red sandstone balconies, latticed screened windows and rooftop *chhatris*. These either face the water or open onto a central garden courtyard. Although the palace is still used as a weekend retreat by the Bikaner royal family, most of the property has now been converted into a luxury hotel known as Dungar Niwas.

ABOVE LEFT The *gomukh* (cow-head) water spout in the Gulab Niwas courtyard.

ABOVE Rajput-styled arcades and European furniture in the central sitting room that opens onto an internal courtyard.

JAISALMER

This remote city in the western extremity of Rajasthan, on the edge of the Thar Desert, owed most of its wealth to the trade caravans that criss-crossed the arid wasteland. Laden with spices, silks, dried fruits and opium from north India and Central Asia, these caravans followed the routes that led to the Arabian Sea ports, from where their goods were shipped to Persia, Arabia and Egypt. This lucrative, trans-desert trade was already fully established by the time Jaisalmer became the headquarters of Rao Jaisal, a Rajput warrior of the Bhati clan. In 1156, Jaisal came upon a great triangular flat-topped hill soaring more than 75 metres above the surrounding sands, on which he built a mud fort, naming it Jaisalmer after himself. Jaisal was succeeded by a number of chiefs who constantly raided each other's territories, but little else is known about these warriors. In 1294, and again shortly afterwards, the Bhatis raided the caravans of Alauddin Khalji, the sultan of Delhi, who retaliated by ordering his troops to sack Jaisalmer Fort, after which it lay abandoned for many years.

During the 15th century, the Bhatis reoccupied Jaisalmer, and continued to rule with some independence from the Delhi sultans. The city and its surrounding territories grew in wealth, partly due to the presence of the Oswal Jain merchants who had prospered from the caravan trade. This favourable situation continued even after north India came under the sway of the Mughals in the mid-16th century. Following the example of their fellow Rajputs, the Bhatis attempted to forge alliances with the Mughals through marriage, beginning with Rawal Bhim Singh (1577-1613) who gave his daughter to Prince Salim, the future Jahangir. The reign of Rawal Sabal Singh (1651-61) marks a significant period in Jaisalmer's history, since he was the first Jaisalmer ruler to formally acknowledge the supremacy of the Mughals, thereby securing some measure of peace and prosperity. The fort in the middle of the city was rebuilt in stone, and the kingdom's territories were extended northwards to the Sutlej River and westward to the Indus. When Sabal Singh attempted to expand his dominions to the east, however, he soon came into conflict with Bikaner. The situation between the two kingdoms deteriorated, and Anup Singh of Bikaner invaded Jaisalmer, though he was eventually repulsed by Rawal Amar Singh (1661-1702), the next Jaisalmer king. Peace was restored with Bikaner only under Rawal Akhai Singh (1722-62). In spite of these disruptions, the city of Jaisalmer continued to grow in wealth, and expanded beyond the fort walls. Due to its isolated location, the state was relatively unaffected by the Maratha incursions that frequently disrupted the other kingdoms of Rajasthan during this period.

During the reign of Maharawal Mul Raj II (1762-1820), portions of the kingdom were lost to Bikaner and Jodhpur, and Baluchi tribes from the Afghan border threatened its western frontier; the state treasury was empty and Jaisalmer was depopulated. The situation was not helped by a prolonged and bitter intrigue between Mul Raj and his scheming prime minister, Swarup Singh. Mul Raj eventually had Swarup beheaded, thereby earning the enmity of his powerful young son, Salim Singh, who inherited the position of prime minister, but plotted the maharawal's downfall. Stability was restored only after 1824, when Salim Singh died after being stabbed by a Rajput noble and then poisoned by his own wife. By this time, the East India Company had already established supremacy in north India, and a treaty had been concluded between the British and Mul Raj in 1818, which guaranteed the succession to his posterity, and protected the Jaisalmer rulers from invasion, provided that they were not the aggressors. After Maharawal Gaj Singh, the grandson of Mul Raj, assumed the throne in 1829, the British forces were called in to help avert a war with Bikaner. Ten years later, Gaj Singh was threatened by Afghan troops, and he once again sought British aid. The East India Company's willingness to support the maharawals is partly explained by its concern to contain Russian influence in the region. In the opinion of James Tod, the British Resident of Udaipur, Jaisalmer's outlying location would be the most practical point of advance into India for the Russians.

Like Bikaner and the Shekhawati region, Jaisalmer was badly affected by the decline of caravan trade in the 19th century. Maharawals Ranjit Singh (1846-64) and Bairi Sal Singh (1864-91) undertook reforms in an attempt to transform their dominions, but the dwindling trans-desert commerce reduced Jaisalmer to an impoverished kingdom that depended largely on earnings from camels, sheep and cattle. Moreover, the severe drought of 1895-1900, during the reign of Maharawal Shalivahan Singh (1891-1914), caused widespread loss of livestock and famine. Attempts at modernization were made by his successor, Maharawal Jawahar Singh (1914-49), but Jaisalmer still remained comparatively backward and isolated. The situation was only rectified after the first paved road was completed in 1958, followed by the railway in 1968. Because of its proximity to the Pakistan border, Jaisalmer is now a major military base. It was at Pokaran, barely 80 kilometres away, that the Indian government tested its first nuclear device in 1974. Brijraj Singh is the current representative of the Jaisalmer family. Supported by the Jaisalmer in Jeopardy trust, he actively campaigns for the protection of the city's remarkable architectural heritage.

PRECEDING PAGES A view of Jaisalmer Fort from the south; its line of ramparts, strengthened by semicircular bastions, protects the houses and palace within.

BELOW Tiers of projecting balconies with tiny *bangla* cornices in Gaj Vilas overlook Dussehra Chowk, the square in front of the fort palace.

JAISALMER FORT PALACE

Located at the highest point within the walls of Jaisalmer Fort, the palace has been the residence of the Bhati rulers since the 15th century. Though the earliest portions of the complex date back to this time, most of its apartments are attributed to the reigns of Maharawals Mul Raj II and Gaj Singh in the frst half of the 19th century. The principal wing, Gaj Vilas, named after its royal founder, faces a public square used for Dussehra celebrations and reviewing troops and animals. Steps to one side of the square ascend to a white marble throne. The palace interior is reached only after passing through a comparatively modest doorway opening off the square. A steep flght of steps gives access to a sequence of apartments arranged in successive levels, with a corridor leading to the adjacent Moti Mahal block. Towards the end of the 19th century, the maharawals shifted to Mandir Palace in the lower city of Jaisalmer; since then the fort palace has stood empty.

ABOVE One of the many yellow stone balconies of the fort palace, carved with geese and cut-out lotus medallions.

ABOVE LEFT Miniature relief patterns in this wall niche in Sarvottam Vilas, an interior apartment, resemble a perforated *jali* screen.

TOP LEFT The Jaisalmer maharawals sat on this marble throne in Dussehra Chowk when reviewing processions of troops and animals.

LEFT A portrait of a European lady is tucked away in one corner of Rang Mahal, a double-height reception room in Jaisalmer Fort Palace.

RIGHT English blue-and-white tiles line the walls of this bedchamber in Gaj Vilas.

FOLLOWING PAGES The courtyard in Moti Mahal is enhanced by a polychrome stone pavement; tiles decorate the lower walls of the side chambers.

BELOW Sarva Niwas, an internal apartment in Mandir Palace, has a central balcony with *bangla* cornices and a dome covered with delicately sculpted designs.

BELOW RIGHT The tower rising over the roof of Mandir Palace comprises two tiers of miniature domed pavilions topped by an octagonal *chhatri*.

MANDIR PALACE

During the course of the 19th century, the Jaisalmer rulers gradually shifted their headquarters from the increasingly cramped and poorly serviced fort palace to Mandir Palace. This dwelling was more conveniently located outside the fort walls, but was still within the walls of the city. Work on this new royal complex began at the beginning of the 19th century at the orders of Maharawal Mul Raj II, and continued into later years under the supervision of Maharawal Bairi Sal Singh. Imitating the *havelis* in the surrounding streets, Mandir Palace is laid out in a sequence of courtyards leading to the private apartments. The stone relief carvings that are a hallmark of the *havelis* are also seen here, but in combination with tile work as in Jaisalmer Fort Palace. Mandir Palace is dominated by a multi-storey tower that offers distant views of Jaisalmer Fort from its arcaded balconies. The palace remains the home of the Jaisalmer royal family to this day, though part of it now functions as a hotel.

LEFT Intricate floral patterns and geometric designs are carved in delicate relief on a wall panel in the inner courtyard.

PATWON KI HAVELI

The reigns of Maharawals Mul Raj II and Gaj Singh, spanning the frst half of the 19th century, witnessed the rise of the Patwas, an Oswal Jain merchant family of Jaisalmer that made its fortune trading in silks, brocades and opium. The Patwas served the maharawals as bankers and councillors, and their elevated status at the Jaisalmer court is revealed in the splendidly appointed Patwon ki Haveli. This mansion was begun in 1805 by Guman Chand, one of the wealthiest representatives of the Oswal family. Like other *havelis* of Jaisalmer, it has multi-storey wings that line a sequence of courts, the innermost one reserved for the private household. Its glory is the street façade, which is almost entirely composed of balconies enclosed with ornately carved windows, arranged in successive tiers. The extraordinarily detailed carved decoration that covers these elements resembles that of woodwork. Part of the *haveli* now houses a crafts emporium and a small museum.

LEFT The elaborate façade of Patwon ki Haveli, wedged between other mansions, rises above this narrow, paved street in Jaisalmer.

251

LEFT The projecting balcony overlooking the inner court of Jaisalmer's Patwon ki Haveli enabled women of the household to observe the proceedings below.

RIGHT The street façade of Patwon ki Haveli presents tiers of balconies with shuttered windows capped by deeply curving *bangla* cornices, all exquisitely carved.

LEFT Disused copper vessels and other utensils are displayed on the kitchen floor in Jaisalmer's Patwon ki Haveli.

ABOVE This room serves as a passage between two wings of the *haveli*.

EPILOGUE

Few palaces in Rajasthan survive intact. Some were abandoned long ago, as at Chittaurgarh, and are now archaeological sites with ruinous and uninhabited monuments, where as other palaces stand in more or less complete condition, though in a state of disrepair as their royal inhabitants have shifted to more conveniently located and better-serviced residences. The dilapidated courtly pavilions at Nagaur Fort have recently been the subject of intense research and rehabilitation, but this is somewhat unusual. After India's independence and the abolishment of princely privileges, it became clear that few Rajput families could afford to maintain their ancestral properties, many which were by this time partly empty and decayed, if not altogether abandoned. Yet royal figures in Rajasthan made every effort to preserve their unique heritage. To this end, most of the families have now set up charitable trusts to channel available financial resources and attract additional funds.

The spectacular growth of the tourist industry in Rajasthan, which at the turn of the 21st century attracted the largest number of international visitors among all the states in India, has provided a positive stimulus to architectural renovation. Today, most of Rajasthan's royal families have transformed their dynastic homes into museums open to the public, as in Jaipur, Udaipur, Jodhpur and Bikaner. Income from visitors, both domestic and international, helps support the ongoing costs of restoration and maintenance. Funds generated in this way also help employ long-standing family retainers who now work as guides and guardians in what have become, in essence, private museums. Redecorated darbar halls, *zenana* wings, garden courtyards and rooftop terraces, as well as family collections of costumes, armour and miniature paintings, remind visitors of the splendour of Rajasthan's past. Such rehabilitation projects have also been made possible because of the surviving skills of local craftsmen who are still able to carve, paint and polish in the traditional manner.

The lure of international tourists has also persuaded some of Rajasthan's royal figures to convert their abandoned but picturesque residences into palace hotels, one of the first being the famous Lake Palace Hotel (Jag Niwas) in Udaipur. Originally a pleasure retreat for the Sisodia rulers and their courtiers, this island resort was almost entirely rebuilt in an imaginative neo-Rajput manner so as to offer luxurious accommodation and modern services. Other royal families were more fortunate since they already had suitably appointed properties that had originally been built as royal guest houses and could easily be outfitted as hotels, the most notable examples being Rambagh Palace in Jaipur and the sprawling Umaid Bhawan in Jodhpur. The former property had originally served as a royal residence; the latter still does to this day. Numerous other families had more modest palaces that still functioned as private residences or vacation resorts. Underused and only partly occupied, many of them have now been converted into hotels, which have sprung up all over Rajasthan, both in the cities as well as more remote locations. Owners often discreetly occupy one of the wings, sometimes even acting as hosts and managers. Such hotels offer visitors the experience of staying in an authentic Rajput environment brimming with furniture, paintings and other paraphernalia that convey the nostalgia for an era that has vanished forever, but which was flourishing barely half a century ago.

While the restoration and renovation of palaces have become major activities over the last two decades, in many instances the work has moved well beyond mere rehabilitation. Genuine looking, but virtually new reception halls, dining rooms, bedroom wings, rooftop terraces and swimming pools have been built around small historical residences all over Rajasthan. Such additions are sometimes carried out with considerable skill so that it is not apparent at first what actually has been added, as in the case of Neemrana Fort Palace. Not only do the exteriors of such properties harmonize successfully with the original core structures, the historic interiors have been entirely reconstituted, complete with expressly purchased and sometimes newly manufactured carpets, hangings, furniture, light fittings and fans. As for oil paintings, photographs, hunting trophies and other mementoes of royal family lives, these may have been specially purchased. In such cases, a consciously recreated atmosphere triumphs over authenticity.

Designers of some rehabilitated palaces are determined to create an idiom that delights in witty references to historical architecture, but which is essentially contemporary in spirit. Nowhere is this better seen than in the palace hotel of Devi Garh in the village of Delwara not far from Udaipur, where Rajput traditions are reconciled with the sleek lines of Modernism. The central block of the neo-Rajput styled hotel of Rajvilas in Jaipur is provided with every Modernist amenity, but is nonetheless a fanciful re-creation of an ancient, mud-clad desert fort. Even the painstaking restoration of Chanwar Palkiwalon ki Haveli, a historical mansion in Amber, outside Jaipur, has not been immune to Modernist innovations. All these projects imaginatively exploit the potentialities of Rajasthan's living craft traditions by employing the techniques of stone and wood carving, inlaid mirror and glass work, and mural painting on specially prepared polished plaster.

NEEMRANA FORT PALACE

Located about 100 kilometres south-west of Delhi, just off the highway to Jaipur, Neemrana Fort Palace dates back to the 15th century, surviving into present times only as a ruinous pile cascading down a steep hillside. From 1986 through the 1990s, the complex was restored and substantially expanded with the addition of new wings, courtyards and terraces. It now functions as a comfortable hotel in an imaginative neo-Rajput style, complete with arcaded reception halls and dining rooms, bedrooms with private balconies, a densely planted garden with a swimming pool, and even a Roman-styled amphitheatre. An outstanding feature of Neemrana Fort Palace is the eclectic style of its different residential suites. While Rajput themes predominate, there is an abundance of furniture and fittings imported from other parts of the country, some of it specially created by India's most talented designers.

PRECEDING PAGES A night view of Neemrana Fort Palace showing the recently added wings and swimming pool.

LEFT Ingeniously crafted wooden tiger chairs greet visitors as they proceed up the ramp, after passing through Chand Pol gateway.

RIGHT Chandra Mahal, the original court room of Neemrana, has been converted into a bedroom suite.

BELOW LEFT A sitting alcove framed in silver-leaf panels in one of the bedroom suites.

BELOW Among the religious imagery introduced by the designer is this cut-out figure of a Jain saviour, fashioned out of gilded wood.

DEVI GARH, DELWARA

Open since 2000, this hotel occupies what had once been a dilapidated palace situated above the village of Delwara in the Aravalli Hills, 28 kilometres north of Udaipur. Towards the end of the 16th century, the Delwara estate was awarded by Rana Pratap Singh of Udaipur to a local warrior chief, Sajja Singh. It was his descendants who built the palace here, most of them occupying the multi-storey *zenana* block in the middle of the complex that grew ever higher over the years. After seven years of extensive restoration, Devi Garh is today a luxurious and imaginatively designed hotel where the past meets the present. The newly refurbished suites exemplify an elegant neo-Rajput idiom, achieved through the use of marble and semi-precious stones, mirror work and inlaid mother-of-pearl, as well as polished plaster work and vividly toned murals. Though following patterns supplied by a young and innovative Indian designer, these materials are handled according to traditional craft techniques.

ABOVE In another bedroom in Devi Garh, garlands of marigolds and mango leaves are painted on the rear wall.

BELOW RIGHT The wall niches have been entirely renewed, though with traditional ochre colouring and white outlines.

BELOW The restoration of the *haveli* involved a painstaking re-creation of the Mughal-inspired arcade that lines the internal court.

CHANWAR PALKIWALON KI HAVELI, AMBER

Once the home of the loyal retainers who waved flywhisks over the heads of the Amber maharajas, Chanwar Palkiwalon ki Haveli is tucked away among the houses of Amber town, in the shadow of the great palace of the Kachhawahas that looms above. Unlike many remodelled properties across Rajasthan that function as hotels today, this previously abandoned and dilapidated mansion has found new life as a cultural and crafts centre. Its interiors are sensitively restored according to traditional building techniques, thereby faithfully recreating the original Rajput character of the building. At the same time, the designers of Chanwar Palkiwalon ki Haveli have managed to explore a distinctive contemporary idiom, in which novel patterns and shapes are fashioned out of polychrome plaster and stone. Such an imaginative, neo-Rajput style forms a perfect setting to the architectural conferences and craft workshops that now take place here.

LEFT Coloured polished stones create bold geometric patterns on the floor.

RAJVILAS, JAIPUR

The traditions of Rajput architecture are continued and enriched in the entirely new resort of Rajvilas, opened in 1997, and located about 8 kilometres east of Jaipur. At the core of the resort is a structure with battlemented walls and bold circular corner towers that emulates the desert forts of Rajasthan. This fort-like structure houses a neo-Rajput styled reception and dining room arranged around a majestic internal courtyard. The accommodations are conceived as separate yet similarly designed buildings located in the more than 12 hectares of landscaped gardens. These gardens are laid out in the fnest Mughal manner, with fountains, lotus pools and domed *chhatri* pavilions, much as in Jaipur's City Palace. The royal suite is a self-contained residence, with its own walled garden and swimming pool. That Rajvilas is built on an old historical site is evident from a small Hindu shrine dating back to the 18th century, as well as a *haveli* belonging to the same period, both standing in the gardens.

LEFT Seats of old bullock carts are reused as lounge chairs beside the swimming pool in the royal suite, with rows of traditional glass globes and lamps hanging from the ceiling.

RIGHT An inlaid polychrome stone walkway with an eight-pointed star design leads from the formal garden to the fortified core block.

GLOSSARY *Restricted to Indian names and terms*

bagh, garden

bala qila, old fort

bangla, pavilion with curving roof and cornices, modelled on a Bengali hut

bhawan (bhavan), hall or apartment

burj, tower

chhatri, domed pavilion; also a royal memorial

chitra shala, painted hall

chowk, courtyard

darbar (durbar), formal reception

Dussehra (Dasara), festival in which the goddess Durga blesses the king's arms, troops and animals

darwaza, gateway

daulat khana, treasury

diwan-i am, hall of public audience

gaddi, cushioned throne

garh, fort; often used in conjunction with descriptive terms such as Juna (old), Lal (red), Loha (iron)

gopi, cow-tending maiden who dances and flirts with Krishna

hammam, steam bath

haveli, mansion

Holi, spring festival

jali, openwork screen

Jats, non-Rajput Hindu rulers in eastern Rajasthan

jharoka, balcony or projecting window

Kachhawaha, ruling house of Jaipur

Krishna, popular, youthful Hindu god who dances and flirts with the *gopis*

Kshatriya, warrior class of Hindu society

mahal, palace or apartment; often used in conjunction with descriptive terms such as Bada (large), Badal (cloud), Chandra (moon), Hawa (breeze), Jal (water), Khas (private), Moti (pearl), Phul (flower), Raj (royal), Rang (colour), Shish (mirror)

maha-, 'great'

maharaja, great king

maharawal, royal title

Malwa, central Indian kingdom ruled from Mandu

mandir, hall; often used in conjunction with descriptive terms such as Jai (victory), Jas (glory), Sukh (pleasure), Vijay (victory)

mardana, male quarters of a palace

Marathas, warrior chiefs from Maharashtra who raided Rajasthan

Marwar, kingdom of Jodhpur

Marwaris, merchant families originating from Shekhawati

Mewar, kingdom of Udaipur

Mughals, supreme emperors of north India from the 16th to the 18th centuries

nawab, Muslim ruler

niwas (nivas), abode or apartment; often used in conjunction with descriptive terms such as Sukh (pleasure), Gulab (rose)

pankha, fan

Parvati, consort of Shiva

pol, gateway; often used in conjunction with descriptive terms such as Chand (moon), Hathi (elephant), Suraj (sun)

puja, Hindu rite of worship

purdah, seclusion of women

Radha, Krishna's favourite *gopi*

Rajputs, warrior clans of Rajasthan and central India

Rama, divine hero considered an incarnation of Vishnu

rana, maharana, title of the Udaipur rulers

rang mahal, palace of colours; frescoed apartment

rao, maharao, royal title

Rathor, ruling house of Jodhpur

rawal, rawat, title of a *thakur*

sagar, samand, lake or pond

sati, ritual act of immolation performed by a Hindu widow after her husband's death

Shekhawati (Shekhavati), region of Rajasthan

shish mahal, mirror palace

Shiva, one of the great cult gods of Hinduism

Sisodia, ruling house of Udaipur

stambha, pillar

thakur, landed noble

tripolia, triple-arched ceremonial gate

vilas, palace or apartment

zenana, female quarters of a palace

BIBLIOGRAPHY

Agarawala, RA. *History, Art & Architecture of Jaisalmer.* Delhi, 1979

—. *Bundi: The City of Painted Walls.* Delhi, 1996

Allen, Charles & Sharada Dwivedi. *Lives of Indian Princes.* London, 1984

Asawa, Gouri Shankar. *Kumbhal Garh: The Invincible Fort.* Jodhpur, 1999

Baroda, Maharaja of & Virginia Fass. *The Palaces of India.* New York, 1980

Barton, Sir William. *The Princes of India.* London, 1934

Bhargava, VS. *Marwar and the Mughal Emperors (AD 1526-1748).* New Delhi, 1966

Bingley, AH. *Handbook on Rajputs.* Reprint, New Delhi, 1986

Cooper, Ilay. *The Painted Towns of Shekhawati.* Ahmedabad, 1994

Crill, Rosemary. *Marwar Painting: A History of the Jodhpur Style.* Mumbai, 1999

Dabas, Bal Krishna. *The Political and Social History of the Jats.* Delhi, 2001

Dave, RK. *Society and Culture of Marwar.* Jodhpur, 1992

Davenport, Hugh. *Trials and Triumphs of the Mewar Kingdom.* Udaipur, 1975

Everyman Guides: Rajasthan. London, 1996

Fass, Virginia. *The Forts of India.* London, 1986

Garde, Anne & Sylvie Raulet. *Maharajas' Palaces: European Style in Imperial India.* London, 1997

Georges, Eliane & Erica Lennard. *Les Petits Palais du Rajasthan.* Paris, 1996

Goetz, Hermann. *The Art and Architecture of Bikaner State.* Oxford, 1950

Goyal, S. *Chittorgarh.* Udaipur, 1983

Gupta, S. *Rajasthan Gazetteer: Jhunjhunu District.* Jaipur, 1984

Hendley, TH. *The Rulers of India and the Chiefs of Rajputana.* London, 1897

Imperial Gazetteers of India, Provincial Series: Rajputana. Reprint, New Delhi, 1989

Jain, Kulbhushan & Minkashi Jain. *Indian City in the Arid West.* Ahmedabad, 1994

Joshi, MC. *Dig.* New Delhi, 1971

Kathuria, RP. *Life in the Courts of Rajasthan during the 18th Century.* New Delhi, 1987

Lethbridge, R. *Chiefs and Leading Families in Rajasthan.* Calcutta, 1916

Lord, John. *The Maharajas.* Reprint, New Delhi, 1989

Master, Brian. *Maharana: The Story of the Rulers of Udaipur.* Ahmedabad, 1990

Michell, George. *The Royal Palaces of India.* London, 1994

Morrow, Ann. *Highness: The Maharajas of India.* New Delhi, 1998

Nand, Sureshwara. *Art & Archaeology of Jaisalmer.* Jodhpur, 2001

Nath, Aman. *Jaipur: The Last Destination.* Bombay, 1993

Nilsson, Sten. *Jaipur: In the Sign of Leo.* Lund, 1987

Pande, Ram. *Bharatpur upto 1826: A Social and Political History of the Jats.* Jaipur, 1970

Patnaik, Naveen. *A Second Paradise: Indian Courtly Life, 1590-1947.* London, 1985

—. *A Desert Kingdom: The Rajputs of Bikaner.* London, 1990

Pinhey, AF. *History of Mewar.* Reprint, Jodhpur, 1996

Robinson, Andrew. *Maharaja: The Spectacular Heritage of Princely India.* New York and London, 1988

Sarkar, Jadunath. *History of Jaipur.* Reprint, Hyderabad, 1984

Sharma, ML. *History of the Jaipur State.* Jaipur, 1969

Sharma, Padma. *Maharaja Man Singh of Jodhpur and his Times.* Agra, 1972

Singh, Dhananajaya. *The House of Marwar: The Story of Jodhpur.* Reprint, New Delhi, 1996

Singh, Harnath. *Shekhawats and their Lands.* Jaipur, 1970

Singh, Karni. *The Relations of the House of Bikaner with the Central Powers.* New Delhi, 1974

Singh, Kishore. *Jodhpur, Bikaner, Jaisalmer: Desert Kingdoms.* New Delhi, 1992

Sugich, M. *Palaces of India*. London, 1992

Tadgell, Christopher. *The History of Architecture in India*. London, 1990

Tillotson, GHR. *The Rajput Palaces: The Development of an Architectural Tradition, 1450-1750*. New Haven and London, 1987

—. *The Tradition of Indian Architecture: Continuity, Controversy and Change Since 1850*. New Haven and London, 1989

Tillotson, GHR & Vibhuti Sachdev. *Building Jaipur: The Making of an Indian City*. London, 2002

Tillotson, Sarah. *Indian Mansions: A Social History of the Haveli*. New Delhi, 1998

Timberg, TA. *The Marwaris*. New Delhi, 1978

Tod, James. *Annals and Antiquities of Rajast'han*. 2 vols. Reprint, New Delhi, 1990

Topsfield, Andrew, ed. *Court Painting in Rajasthan*. Mumbai, 2001

Wacziarg, Francis & Aman Nath. *Rajasthan: The Painted Walls of Shekhavati*. London, 1982

Welch, Stuart Cary, ed. *Gods, Kings, and Tigers: The Art of Kotah*. Munich and New York, 1997

Wolwahsen, Andreas. *Cosmic Architecture in India: The Astronomical Observatories of Maharaja Jai Singh II*. Munich, London and Ahmedabad, 2001

ACKNOWLEDGEMENTS

Together with Antonio Martinelli, I wish to acknowledge the contribution of Aman Nath, who generously made available his specialist knowledge on Rajasthan's history and culture. Thanks to his introductions, I was able to benefit from information provided by a number of key figures: namely, Gayatri Devi of Jaipur; Gaj Singh of Jodhpur; Brijraj Singh of Kotah; Arvind Singh of Mewar; Narendra Singh of Jaipur; Mohan Singh of Kanota; Ram Pratap Singh of Diggi; Sanjai Singh of Bissau; Yadavendra Singh of Samode; Randhir Vikram Singh of Mandawa; Devendra Singh of Nawalgarh; Ranbir Sinh and Raghuvendra Singh (Bonnie) of Dundlod; Rajendra and Surendra Singh of Shahpura; Jitendra Singh and Ambika of Alwar; Vishvendra Singh and Divya Kumari of Bharatpur; Hemant Singh and Dushyant Singh of Dholpur; Shatrunjai Singh and Bhavna Kumari of Deogarh; Sunder Singh of Bambora; Randhir Singh of Bijaipur; Hemendra Singh of Bhainsrorgarh; Harshvardhan Singh of Dungarpur; Usha Devi of Jodhpur; Rajvir Singh of Luni; Rajyashree of Bikaner and Dalip Singh; Mahendra Singh and Sunder Singh, Jodhpur; BS Auwa, Udaipur; Sunil Kumar Rampuria, Bikaner; Bindu Manchanda for Jaisalmer; Lekha and Anupam Poddar, Devi Garh; Nimish Patel, Ahmadabad; and Paul Jones, Rajvilas.

The following scholars outside India have also been encouraging and helpful: Joachim Bautze, Joan Bowers, Ilay Cooper, Richard Runnels and Andrew Topsfield.

I would also like to thank the expert editorial and design team led by Meera Ahuja at IBH, which worked hard to ensure that the book is successfully completed.

— **GEORGE MICHELL**, London

Sincere support came from PN Nageshwaran and Ramesh Raghavan of Incent Tours in Delhi, who organized and provided travel facilities and advice for the long photographic campaign in Rajasthan. Didier Sandman of La Route des Indes also contributed to my trips from Paris.

I am also indebted to my photographic assistant, Malkhan Singh from Neemrana, who shared with me good and bad times with genuine enthusiasm all through the long journey.

Prithvi Singh offered me hospitality at Narain Niwas, and made me feel at home during my long stay in Jaipur. I would like to thank him and his family as well as all the staff members of Narain Niwas Palace Hotel and Raj Mahal Palace Hotel.

Among others, I would like to thank Francis Wacziarg and Aman Nath as well as all the staff of Neemrana Fort-Palace, Piramal Haveli and Kesroli Fort.

In Rajasthan I was graciously welcomed, and received generous hospitality from Sunil Kumar and Prashant Rampuria, Bhanwar Niwas Hotel, Bikaner; Kirti Kumar Mathur (General Manager), Lallgarh Palace WelcomHeritage Hotel, Bikaner; Jaidev Singh (Manager), Gajner Palace Hotel; Raghuraj Singh (Managing Director), Shiv Raj Singh and Deep Raj, Laxmi Vilas Palace Hotel, Bharatpur; Narendra Singh and Randhir Singh (Managing Director), Hotel Pratap Palace, Chittaurgarh and Castle Bijaipur; Rajveer Singh, Fort Chanwa, Luni; Nahar Singh and Shatrunjai Singh Chundawat, Deogarh Mahal; Raghuvir Singh and Raghuvendra Singh, Dundlod; Priyadarshini and Harshvardhan Singh, Udai Bilas Palace, Dungarpur.

In Jaipur, Narendra Singh and the royal family, City Palace; RD Singh (General Manager), Raj Mahal Palace Hotel; Rahul Pahwa (Sales Manager), Jai Mahal (Taj); Ram Rathore, Rambagh Palace Hotel (Taj); Peter Dessa for Ramgarh Lodge; Ram Pratap Singh, Hotel Diggi Palace; Yadavendra Singh and Lalit Singh Sisodia, Samode Haveli and Samode Palace. Jitendra Singh, Jawahar Niwas Palace, Jaisalmer; Gaj Singh of Jodhpur, Sunder Singh (Director Marketing) and Vimi Mathur (Manager Guest Relations), Umaid Bhawan Palace, Jodhpur; Avijit Sen (Manager), Balsamand Lake Palace; Chetan Bhatnagar (Resident Manager), Ajit Bhawan, Jodhpur; Onkar Singh and Gajendra Singh, New Palace Hotel, Khimsar; Brijraj Singh of Kotah; Vijender Singh (General Manager), Umed Bhawan Palace, Kota; Kesri Singh (Director), Hotel Castle Mandawa; Dinesh Dhabhai, Mandawa Haveli; Yatendra Singh (Manager), Roop Niwas Palace, Nawalgarh; Manish Sharma (Duty Manager), Sawai Madhopur Lodge, Ranthambhor; Ajay Pal Singh (Manager), Rawla Narlai; Rao Rajendra Singh, Shahpura; Arvind Singh of Mewar; Raj Lakshmi and Harshala Ghorpade (Business Development Executive), HRH Group of Hotels and Rathore (Assistant Manager), Fateh Prakash Palace, Udaipur.

I would like to specially thank Gayatri Devi of Jaipur for allowing me to photograph Lilypool.

Others who facilitated access to the palaces were: Jitendra Singh of Alwar; John Singh, Chanwar Palkiwalon ki Haveli, Amber; Sunder Singh, Karni Fort, Bambora; Shiv Charan Singh Chundawat, Rajveer Singh Chundawat and Hemendra Singh Chundawat, Bhainsrorgarh; Praveen Shelley (General Manager), Laxmi Niwas Palace, Bikaner; Rajyashree of Bikaner and Dalip Singh (Co-ordinator), Maharaja Ganga Singhji Trust, Bikaner; Vishvendra Singh of Bharatpur; Ranjit Singh of Bundi; Sanjai Singh of Bissau; Brijraj Singh of Jaisalmer; Raghuveer Singh Bhati (Director), Fort Palace Museum, Jaisalmer; Nand Kishore Mohta, Patwon ki Haveli, Jaisalmer; Jugal Joshi, Craft Palace, Jaisalmer; Mahendra Singh (Chief Executive Officer) and Jitendra Singh Awwa (Director), Mehrangarh Museum Trust, Jodhpur; Sawai Singh Shekhawat, Poddar Haveli Museum, Nawalgarh; M Umar Khan and RA Maulana Abul Kalam Azad, Arabic and Persian Research Institute, Tonk; Amrendu Dholakia (Duty Manager), Lake Palace Hotel (Taj), Udaipur; Bhupendra Singh (Chief Administrator), City Palace Museum, Udaipur.

Special thanks goes to Aradhana Nagpal of India Book House who perfectly organized all contacts with the owners of the palaces all over Rajasthan.

Permission to photograph protected sites and monuments was granted by KP Poonacha (Director of Monuments), Archaeological Survey of India, New Delhi; RC Agrawal, Indian Council of Historic Research (ICHR), Ministry of Human Resources, New Delhi; and Akshay Jagdari (Director of Archaeology and Museums), State Archaeology Department, Government of Rajasthan, Jaipur.

In France, I benefited from the help of Sanjay Panda (Cultural Secretary) and Nilanjana Ray at the Ambassade de l'Inde. Massimo Giacometti, Corinne Bunzl and Peter Martinelli Bunzl must be specially thanked for their support and help.

All the photographs were taken with over-abused Nikon equipment on Kodachrome slides processed at the Kodak lab in Lausanne, supervised by Sandro Marsili. They were carried back to India by Marie-Christine Bertrand, to whom I owe a special debt.

— **ANTONIO MARTINELLI**, Paris

ILLUSTRATED PALACE INDEX

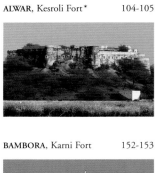

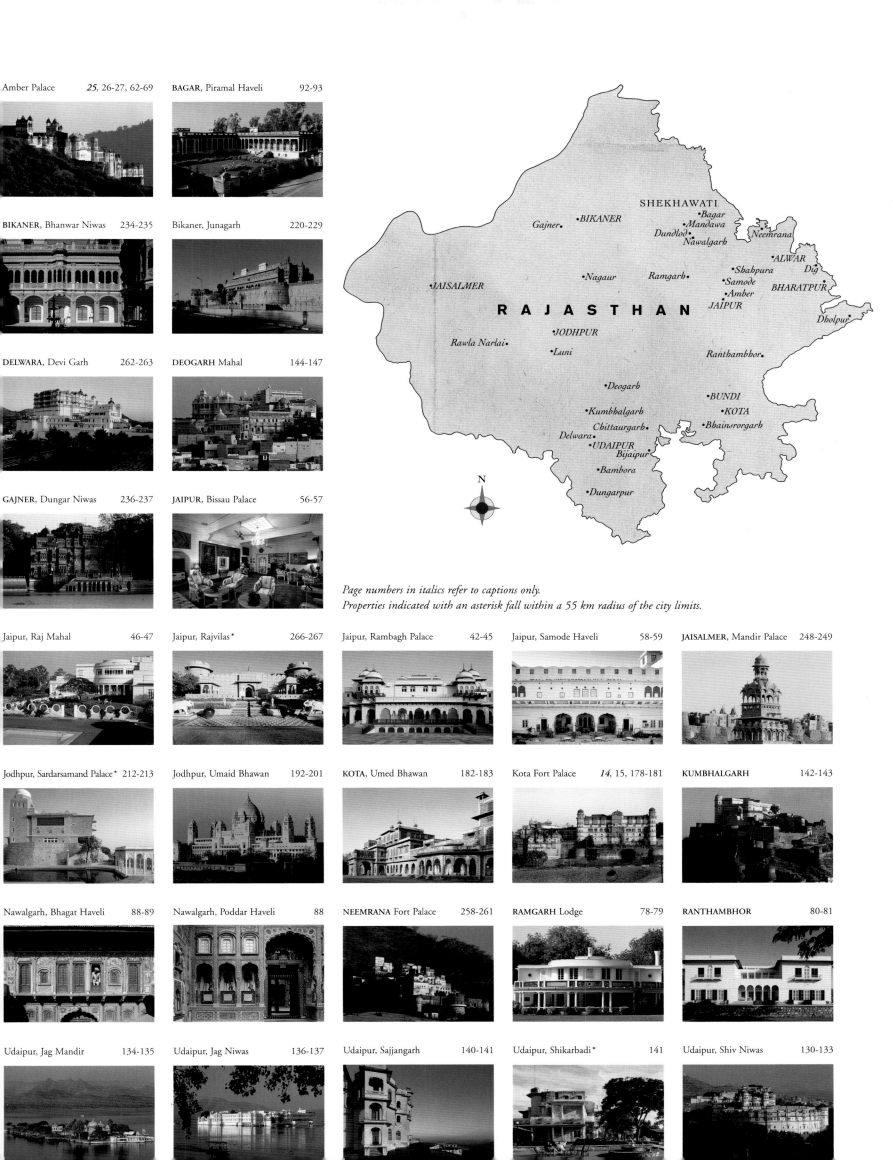
Page numbers in italics refer to captions only.
Properties indicated with an asterisk fall within a 55 km radius of the city limits.

First published in the United States of America by
The Vendome Press
1334 York Avenue
New York, NY 10021

First published in India by
India Book House Pvt Ltd
Text © George Michell, 2004
Photographs © Antonio Martinelli, 2004

Design: Anne Marie Koster

ISBN: 0-86565-2406

Library of Congress Cataloging-in-Publication Data

Michell, George.
    Princely Rajasthan : Rajput palaces and mansions / George
Michell; photographs by Antonio Martinelli.
    p. cm.
    Includes bibliographical references and index.
    ISBN 0-86565-240-6 (hardcover : alk. paper)
    1. Architecture, Rajput–India–Rajasthan. 2.
Palaces–India–Rajasthan. 3. Mansions–India–Rajasthan.
I. Martinelli, Antonio. II. Title.
NA1507.R35M53 2004
728.8'2'09544–dc22   2004043053

Photo Credits: pp. 118-119 © Anne Garde; pp. 262-263
© Henry Wilson

Printed in China